40.70

DATE DUE

MAY 0 9 2000	

DEMCO, INC. 38-2931

CI OGY

ALBRE
BEUTE

CRYPTOLOGY

ALBRECHT BEUTELSPACHER

An introduction to the Art and Science of Enciphering, Encrypting, Concealing, Hiding and Safeguarding
Described
Without any Arcane Skullduggery
but not
Without Cunning Waggery
for the
Delectation and Instruction
of the General Public
by
Albrecht Beutelspacher

Transformation from German into English
Succored and Abetted
by J. Chris Fisher

The Mathematical Association of America

Originally published in the German language by Friedr. Vieweg &
Sohn Verlagsgesellschaft mbH, D-6200 Wiesbaden, Federal Republic of
Germany, under the title "Kryptologie. 2. Auflage (2nd Edition)".
Copyright 1991 by Friedr. Vieweg & Sohn Verlagsgesellschaft mbH,
Braunschweig/Wiesbaden.

ISBN 0-88385-504-6

Printed in the United States of America

Current printing (last digit):
10 9 8 7 6 5 4 3 2

MAA Service Center, P.O. Box 90973, Washington, DC 20036
1-800-331-1MAA   FAX: 1-301-206-9789

INTRODUCTION

> A bard will wish to profit or to please
> Or, as a tertium quid, do both of these.
>
> —Horace, *De Arte Poetica*
> (the Conington translation)

As long as there are creatures endowed with language, there will be confidential communication—messages intended for a limited audience. How can these messages be transmitted secretly, so that *no unauthorized person gets knowledge of the content of a message*? And how can one guarantee that a message arrives in the right hands exactly as it was transmitted?

Traditionally, there are two ways to answer such questions. One can disguise the very existence of a message, perhaps by writing with invisible ink; or try to transmit the message via a trustworthy person. This is the method favored throughout history by clandestine lovers—and nearly all classical tragedies provide evidence of the method's shortcomings.

A totally different approach is to *encipher* (or *encrypt*) a message. In this case one does not disguise its existence. On the contrary, the message is transmitted over a public, insecure channel, but encrypted in such a way that no one except the intended recipient may decipher it. This offers a rather tempting challenge to an enemy. Such challenges are usually accepted—and not unusually overcome.

In this book I deal mainly with the latter approach, enciphering messages. I also examine the closely related topic of the integrity and authenticity of data, where the aim is not to protect messages against unauthorized reading but against unauthorized altering.

Until some years ago sophisticated, secure systems were restricted primarily to the military world. Only the military had sufficient motivation and resources to produce sophisticated mechanical coding devices. One particularly famous machine was the ENIGMA (Greek for mystery), which was widely used by the Germans during World War II. This machine, like its American counterpart (the M-209), was an admirable technological miracle. Systematic attacks on ENIGMA-enciphered messages were successfully executed mainly at two places: before the war in Poland and, in the early forties, at Bletchley Park (UK). The English were not only able to break the ENIGMA code but were apparently also successful in keeping the Germans unaware of this fact during the war. (Another machine, the *Geheimschreiber* T-52 of Siemens and Halske, remained secure throughout the war.)

There is a bridge from the cryptanalytic efforts of the English to the origins of modern data processing. During World War II the British developed electromechanical and electronic tools to break the German codes. The most famous machine, the COLOSSUS, can be seen as the first digital computer. It is to be noted, however, that the English mathematician Alan M. Turing (1912–1954), who later became one of the founders of computer science, played a central role in the Bletchley Park decoding group—yet surprisingly was not directly involved in the development of the COLOSSUS.

There is a satisfying appropriateness to cryptology's role in the birth of electronic computing. With the overwhelming propagation of electronic data processing since the sixties, cryptology has itself been reborn. Several reasons for this rebirth come quickly to mind.

- When breaking a cryptosystem, one has to process huge sets of data (long strings of letters and enormous numbers). One has to compare data, compute means and standard deviations, and much more—all things that a computer does with far greater speed and reliability than a human being. Consequently, today's cryptosystems must be much more sophisticated than their predecessors of only fifty years ago in order to withstand cryptanalytic attacks.
- On the other hand, the development of computer technology permits the implementation of complex and sophisticated mathematical algorithms, which attain a degree of security unparalleled in history. A small increase in a code's complexity leads to a spectacular increase

in the resources needed to break the system. Here is a theme that recurs throughout this book: not only is the computer the cause of a great many problems, it is, ironically, also the key to their solution.

- As electronic data processing permeates more and more areas of endeavor—in particular those where electronic communication is involved—there arise completely new areas of application for cryptology, often far from its classical military roots.

One does not need a crystal ball to predict that cryptology (which only recently became accepted as a science) will experience even more rapid growth. Some typical new applications follow.

- Many phone calls are processed via satellite. It is easy to listen in on such conversations. Consequently, sensitive phone calls must be encrypted.
- A rather similar problem—the unauthorized viewer—arises with respect to pay TV. By means of cryptology-based user authentication (to be discussed in chapter 4) one can foil any spongers.
- Similarly, in a multiuser computer system, each user must be identified. Today this is accomplished using passwords; in the future, at least for top-security applications, the use of a "smart card" that provides a much higher level of security will be required.
- With the increasing use of electronic banking comes the need to find a good substitute for the handwritten signature. In many ways the so-called electronic signature successfully supersedes the ordinary signature (see chapter 5).
- A final application to be mentioned here concerns computer viruses. These are little parts of a program introduced from an outside computer; they have the ability to reproduce themselves, resulting in great harm to programs, data, and even whole systems. Roughly speaking, a virus alters a program without authorization. So, methods of data authentication (to be discussed in chapters 4 and 5) might be considered a means of defense against viruses.

After considering these and other potential applications, everyone will agree and say, "Of course, we need security! But why is cryptology the recommended remedy? Aren't there other ways to achieve security?" Of course, there are! Think, for instance, of the elaborate techniques developed over the centuries for making our banknotes secure: special paper, intricate (sometimes beautiful) pictures, precision printing, watermarks, special silver wires, and so on. So, really, why cryptology?

The answer is simple: *Cryptology is better.* One reason: *Cryptology is a mathematical discipline!* Perhaps this sounds exaggerated. But mathematics provides—at least in principle—the theoretical justification behind the strength of a particular algorithm or protocol. Mathematics can *prove* that a given algorithm is secure. Once security has been proved mathematically, there can be no doubt that the algorithm is secure; there is no need to rely on experts' (often contradictory) opinions, no need to base one's judgement on the state of "today's technology," and so forth.

It must be mentioned that such proofs have been achieved in only a very few cases. Nonetheless, mathematics provides a reliable means for systematically investigating—that is, analyzing and designing—crypto algorithms, and this is reason enough to prefer cryptologic mechanisms over other security systems.

The science that deals with all the aforementioned problems is called by either of two names, *cryptology* or *cryptography.* I present those parts of cryptology that, in my opinion, are important for the understanding of modern developments. In other words, this book contains that part of cryptology that belongs to a liberal arts education. Of course, such a goal cannot be achieved without, from time to time, considering a system in detail ("getting one's hands dirty," as we say in the trade). But my guiding principle has been to produce a *readable* book that presents material as clearly as possible, avoiding unnecessary formalities.

The first chapter has two aims. First, I present some of the classical monoalphabetic ciphers over the natural alphabet. (It will turn out that these ciphers can be broken without great difficulty.) Second, I introduce the fundamental cryptologic notions and terminology.

The second chapter is devoted to polyalphabetic ciphers. These are more sophisticated and, hence, require more sophisticated methods for breaking them. Two such methods are considered in detail.

The third chapter is a theoretical discussion. There the reader will find the definitions needed to investigate cipher systems and perfect cipher systems. Also I discuss examples such as the one-time pad. In the second half of this chapter I discuss shift registers, which are the basis for many modern algorithms.

In the fourth chapter I deal with integrity and authenticity. In this part of cryptology the aim is not to conceal messages but to code them in such a way that one can guarantee that they reach their destination without any alteration, be it accidental or malevolent. This is the application responsible for lifting cryptology during the past twenty years from the limited realm of the military to its lofty position in the world of commerce. (An example will make the importance of this application obvious. It is not the end of the world if a hostile party knows how much money is transferred from the university to my account every month; but if he is capable of altering the amount or the account number on the check without being detected, I most likely would react in an unfriendly manner!) In this chapter I present also the exciting news of the so-called zero-hyphen- knowledge protocol (can I convince you to have a secret without revealing it?) which attracted great interest, both from a theoretical and from a practical point of view during the last year. I also briefly discuss smart cards, which are *the* means of providing cryptographic-based security to individuals.

In the fifth chapter I introduce and discuss in some detail the famous public-key systems, whose introduction by Diffie and Hellman in 1976 began a revolution in cryptology. One measure of this revolution is the subsequent acceptance of cryptology as an important branch of mathematics. But the elegance of public-key cryptology provides something more than a plaything for mathematicians: it promises to be very practical, which indeed was the reason for its invention.

In the final chapter I consider anonymity, a phenomenon that is perhaps a bit outside the usual scope of cryptology. In fact, I know of no other book on the subject where this topic is broached. In most computer-based systems security is provided, in a large part, by auditing—that is, keeping track of all relevant data. Thus, every relevant event is reconstructible and nothing is kept secret. So the computer, somewhat like God, knows everything. Is it possible to design electronically-based systems (for instance, for electronic shopping) that are not quite so omniscient—providing security on the one hand and anonymity on the other? I discuss two proposals for anonymity. In particular I discuss whether there is a practical electronic analogue to our ordinary coins.

These topics are new, exciting, and very practical. Perhaps such comments bring on a fear that everything will become very complicated and esoteric. Don't worry! Cryptology isn't like that; it should be possible to explain the new and futuristic themes very clearly and simply. Anyway, such was my goal.

There is no need to read the chapters in the natural order. Don't be alarmed if one or another passage appears cryptic. Usually subsequent text will be understandable without having understood a particular difficult passage; obscure sentences tend to clarify themselves in time. My advice: Skip over a page from time to time—and do so without remorse.

I do hope that the reader will enjoy this book. I tried to compromise between the military's approach to these topics—they tend to take these things too seriously—and the general public's—they tend to take these things too lightly. One youthful critic of the book's first edition reports that she kept her copy beside the bathtub; she found it made stimulating reading while bathing. I couldn't have hoped for a better reaction.

This book is not simply a translation of the German original. It is, rather, a new edition designed for an English-speaking audience. Although the structure and intent have remained, there are new topics in every chapter that take into account recent developments.

Finally, I have the pleasure to thank the many people who have supported this project—too many to name them all.

First I thank my nearest relatives Monika, Christoph, and Maria. Not only did I use them quite frequently as guinea pigs, but they generously granted me vacations in order to write this book.

Also, I thank my colleagues A, F, I, L, M, and U (in alphabetical order, where several letters count more than once), who supported this book in various ways: reading, criticizing, suggesting alterations, inspiring me by their presence, providing additional material, taking over some of my duties, and much more.

Last but not least (which is *true* in this case), I have to mention my friend Chris Fisher. He simply refused to produce a plain translation of the book. Directly and indirectly he demanded such drastic alterations (under the guise of the phrase "I don't understand this") that he urged me to write a completely new book. Thank you!

Some Technical Comments

At the end of each chapter you will find exercises—more than 100 in all. All of the exercises are fun (I hope) and most of them are easy. (Hint: The more difficult ones are made easy by giving you a hint.)

Exercises that are likely to take some time are marked with a ▷. You will also find quite a few programming exercises; they are marked with the "at" symbol @. As always, programming exercises demand time.

Since a good part of modern cryptology is based on properties of integers, we shall have to use the mod notation. This is easy. Given two positive integers a and b, we denote by

$$a \bmod b$$

the remainder obtained by dividing b into a. Thus $a \bmod b$ is always a number less than b; for example,

$$1 \bmod 5 = 6 \bmod 5 = 41 \bmod 5 = 1$$

(i.e., the remainder is 1);

$$1992 \bmod 4 = 0$$

(i.e., 4 divides evenly into 1992), and so forth.

CONTENTS

Chapter 1

CAESAR
or
THE BEGINNING IS EASY

Opi lopove yopou
Lopottope, sopo mopuch.
Dopo yopou opalsopo
Lopove mope? Nopo, soporropy.

Nopear opor fopar
Mopay Gopod bope wopith yopou.
Mopy hopeart topook plopeasopure
Opin yopour copompopanopy.

—Joachim Ringelnatz

It is seldom easy to be young and in love. We learn from great literature that when Juliet dispatches a confidential message to her beloved Romeo, there is almost always an antagonist wanting to intercept it. Perhaps the villain wishes only to read the message. The remedy against such a *passive attack* is encryption, the subject of this and three of the next four chapters. Against an *active attack*, where the bad guy is out to alter the message (presumably in some insidious way), Juliet would be advised to turn to the fourth and fifth chapters, which are devoted to authentication and data integrity.

The moral of the story for lovers (as well as for soldiers, yuppies, and anyone else who has a confidential message to send) is that it is necessary to consider countermeasures to foil the bad guy, or at least to make his job as tough as possible. To do this one might use a cipher. In that case Juliet

1

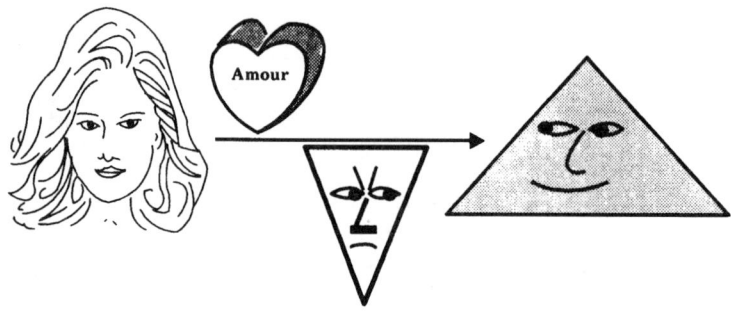

FIGURE 1.1
A passive attack

would replace each letter of each word by another letter (or an appropriate symbol such as a number).

Whatever the cipher, the recipient must know more about it than any attacker knows. With that information, the recipient can decipher the message; without it the attacker is foiled (or at least set back). This exclusive information is called the *key*. Classical cipher systems are *symmetric*: sender and recipient share a secret key. In chapter 5 we shall see that asymmetric cipher systems exist also; in those systems only the recipient needs to have a secret key.

In this chapter we look at simple systems in which each letter of the alphabet has a single replacement letter. For instance, the letter **x** of the message could be enciphered by the code letter **A**. By the end of this chapter the reader should have learned that such systems are not particularly secure.

Let us start with some remarks concerning terminology. The words *cryptology* and *cryptography* come from the Greek κρψπτοσ (hidden), λογοσ (word or reason), and γραφια (writing). They have the same meaning, namely, the art and science of designing methods in order to disguise messages. (Some authors distinguish between *cryptography*, the science of designing ciphersystems; *cryptanalysis*, the art of breaking those systems; and *cryptology*, which comprises both parts.)

The message (the sequence of letters or symbols which we want to transmit) is called the *cleartext* (or *plaintext*). I shall usually represent the cleartext by boldface lowercase letters such as **a, b, c,** .... The enciphered message (the sequence of letters and symbols that is in fact transmitted) is called the *ciphertext*, which will be denoted by boldface uppercase letters **A, B, C,** .... The process of transforming cleartext to ciphertext is called *enciphering* (or *encrypting* or *encoding*—although the last term does not carry the connotation of secrecy imparted by the other two words); the inverse operation is called *deciphering*. Therefore, the *sender* enciphers a cleartext, whereas the recipient must decipher the ciphertext in order to obtain an intelligible message.

A *cipher* is the system of all cleartexts, the corresponding ciphertexts, and the rule which assigns to any cleartext a ciphertext (see chapter 3). The messages we consider are composed of letters, which form the elements of an *alphabet*. In the first two chapters our alphabet will usually be the natural alphabet $\{a, b, c, \ldots\}$. But if it is suitable for our purposes we shall also consider other alphabets, for instance, the set $\{1, \ldots, 26\}$, the set $\{0, 1\}$, or even the set $\{(a_1, \ldots, a_{64}) \mid a_i \in \{0, 1\}\}$ of all binary sequences of length 64.

Despite the implication of this chapter's title, our topic predates Caesar.

1.1 THE SPARTAN SCYTALE

This story begins about 2500 years ago. According to the Greek biographer Plutarch, the Spartan government sent secret messages to its generals in the following clever way. Sender and recipient each had a cylinder—called a *scytale* (pronounced SITalee)—of exactly the same radius. The sender wound a narrow ribbon of parchment around his cylinder, then wrote on it *lengthwise* (see Figure 1.2). After the ribbon had been unwound, the writing could be read only by a person who had a cylinder of exactly the same circumference—the intended recipient, let us hope.

Consider an example in modern language. Suppose we have intercepted a strip of paper that bears the following sequence of letters.

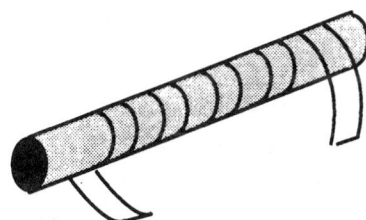

FIGURE 1.2
A scytale

SYBLCRESEERACHTAYPUOHIPHRUEMTY
ILSOO!TDOFG

The scytale used by the sender has a circumference c, which we may measure by the number of letters. So, we may simply try several circumferences c. If we try $c = 5$, and rearrange our message in five columns, we get complete nonsense, as follows.

S	R	R	A	H	U	I	!	G
Y	E	A	Y	I	E	L	T	
B	S	C	P	P	M	S	D	
L	E	H	U	H	T	O	O	
C	E	T	O	R	Y	O	F	

However, if we arrange it in $c = 6$ columns, the message becomes clear.

S	E	C	U	R	I	T
Y	S	H	O	U	L	D
B	E	T	H	E	S	O
L	E	A	I	M	O	F
C	R	Y	P	T	O	G
R	A	P	H	Y	!	

The scytale is the prototype of a *transposition cipher*, in which the letters remain what they are, but not where they were. Mathematically a transposition cipher can be described as a permutation of the *positions* of the letters. Many popular cryptographic algorithms are based on transposition ciphers (see, for instance, exercises 3 and 23). Also, chapter 3 of [Smi71] has a large selection of classical transposition ciphers.

Transposition ciphers provide an important building block for modern algorithms. The other ingredients are the *substitution ciphers*, in which each letter of the cleartext is replaced by another letter, but it keeps its position. Here is where Caesar enters the stage.

1.2 ADDITIVE CIPHERS

An early user of cryptographic techniques was the famous Roman commander-in-chief and statesman Gaius Julius Caesar (100–44 B.C.). In the second century A.D. Suetonius wrote (*Lives of the Caesars LVI*):

There exist also [letters from Caesar] to Cicero and acquaintances on topics on which he, when he had to transmit them confidentially, wrote in cipher. That is he changed the order of letters in such a way that no word could be made out. If somebody wanted to decipher it and understand the content, then he had to insert the fourth letter of the alphabet, that is D, for A, and so on.

We obtain Caesar's cipher if we write the ciphertext alphabet beneath the cleartext alphabet—shifted by twenty-three positions to the right or, equivalently, three positions to the left.

Cleartext: a b c d e f g h i j k l m n o p q r s t u v w x y z
Ciphertext: D E F G H I J K L M N O P Q R S T U V W X Y Z A B C

We encipher a cleartext letter by replacing it by the letter beneath it. For instance, **cleartext** becomes **FOHDUWHAW**. Deciphering is equally easy; we must replace a ciphertext letter by the cleartext letter above it. So, for example, **OHWWHU** is deciphered to **letter**.

The reader would be justified in asking why Caesar shifted the ciphertext alphabet by three letters. The answer is simple: there is no reason. We may of course shift the second alphabet by any number of positions. Since our alphabet consists of twenty-six letters, we obtain exactly twenty-six such ciphers. They are called *additive ciphers*. (The reason for this name is explained in section 1.4.) Among these ciphers, there is also the *trivial* cipher $a \rightarrow A, b \rightarrow B, \ldots, z \rightarrow Z$, which was probably never used for reasons of secrecy. Table 1.1 shows all twenty-six additive ciphers.

Of course, it is still somewhat tedious to encipher long texts using such a table. In 1470, the Renaissance architect and theorist Leone Battista Alberti (1404–1472) invented a machine based on two discs that mechanized the enciphering process. Figure 1.3 shows a machine that realizes all twenty-six additive ciphers. The inner disc may be rotated against the outer disc, resulting in any additive cipher that one wishes. Enciphering and deciphering is then a piece of cake! By means of this simplest class of ciphers we can clarify two extremely important notions, the cipher algorithm and the actual key. One should carefully distinguish between them. The *algorithm* for an additive cipher can be described by Table 1.1, or equally well by the machine shown in Figure 1.3; it is the *computational procedure*, the recipe that, when followed carefully, enciphers and deciphers messages. On the other hand, the *key* is, for instance, the number of positions the ciphertext

Cleartext: a b c d e f g h i j k l m n o p q r s t u v w x y z

```
A B C D E F G H I J K L M N O P Q R S T U V W X Y Z
B C D E F G H I J K L M N O P Q R S T U V W X Y Z A
C D E F G H I J K L M N O P Q R S T U V W X Y Z A B
D E F G H I J K L M N O P Q R S T U V W X Y Z A B C
E F G H I J K L M N O P Q R S T U V W X Y Z A B C D
F G H I J K L M N O P Q R S T U V W X Y Z A B C D E
G H I J K L M N O P Q R S T U V W X Y Z A B C D E F
H I J K L M N O P Q R S T U V W X Y Z A B C D E F G
I J K L M N O P Q R S T U V W X Y Z A B C D E F G H
J K L M N O P Q R S T U V W X Y Z A B C D E F G H I
K L M N O P Q R S T U V W X Y Z A B C D E F G H I J
L M N O P Q R S T U V W X Y Z A B C D E F G H I J K
M N O P Q R S T U V W X Y Z A B C D E F G H I J K L
N O P Q R S T U V W X Y Z A B C D E F G H I J K L M
O P Q R S T U V W X Y Z A B C D E F G H I J K L M N
P Q R S T U V W X Y Z A B C D E F G H I J K L M N O
Q R S T U V W X Y Z A B C D E F G H I J K L M N O P
R S T U V W X Y Z A B C D E F G H I J K L M N O P Q
S T U V W X Y Z A B C D E F G H I J K L M N O P Q R
T U V W X Y Z A B C D E F G H I J K L M N O P Q R S
U V W X Y Z A B C D E F G H I J K L M N O P Q R S T
V W X Y Z A B C D E F G H I J K L M N O P Q R S T U
W X Y Z A B C D E F G H I J K L M N O P Q R S T U V
X Y Z A B C D E F G H I J K L M N O P Q R S T U V W
Y Z A B C D E F G H I J K L M N O P Q R S T U V W X
Z A B C D E F G H I J K L M N O P Q R S T U V W X Y
```

TABLE 1.1
The twenty-six additive ciphers

alphabet has been shifted, or the position of the discs, or the ciphertext equivalent of the letter **a**, and so forth; the key tells precisely *how the algorithm proceeds* in a particular message. Sender and recipient first must agree on a cipher algorithm and then, before any transmission, choose and exchange their key.

Here some remarks are in order. The algorithm and the key have totally different functions. As a rule, the algorithm is rather large. (Many algorithms are realized by a mechanical or electronic device, or are based on a complex mathematical procedure.) As a consequence, the algorithm cannot be kept secret. This means that the *overall security of a cryptosystem relies on the secrecy of the key.*

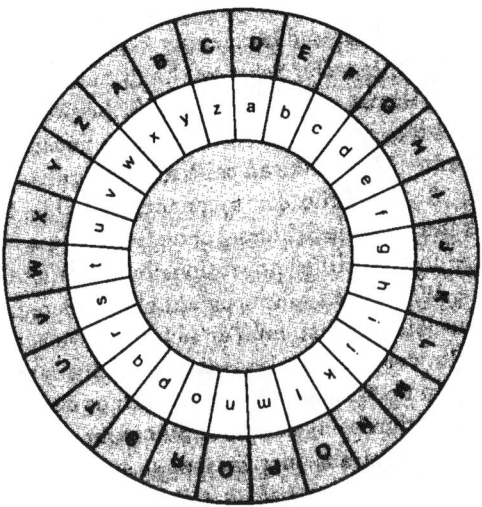

FIGURE 1.3
An enciphering machine

This statement may seem exaggerated, but in fact it is not. The determined bad guy who wants to read our message can, with relative ease, obtain the algorithm (for example, a machine). Fortunately (one hopes!) he still does not know the current key.

As an important consequence, the key must be transmitted securely. Pardon? Isn't this nonsense? Why not dispense with the key and simply transmit the message using this secret channel? This objection is quite justified. But consider the following arguments.

- As a rule, messages can be very long. In contrast, the key will be short (that is, as short as justifiable with respect to security). Therefore, the effort in securely transmitting the key is very limited. The probability that the bad guy intercepts the key is thus relatively small.
- Sender and recipient may choose the moment of key exchange. The exchange can take place days, even weeks or months before the transmission of the message. In contrast, the message often has to be transmitted at a time that is beyond the sender's control. (Think of political events, unexpected developments in the stock market, and so on.)
- Using so-called public key cryptosystems (see chapter 5), one can exchange a key even without a secret channel.

In this context we note another danger. Once the key has been exchanged, it must not be possible to read the key out of the machine. Many experts claim that a key can be stored secretly only if it is protected by physical means.

Now the time has come to change sides. Cryptology consists not only of the design of algorithms and systems for keeping messages secret; one of the central aims in cryptology is also to break these systems—or at least to try.

Let us, therefore, play the bad guy's role. To express this less euphemistically: We work as a *cryptanalyst* and try to perform a *cryptanalysis* of a given ciphertext (or of the cryptosystem in question). The designer of a cryptosystem always has to take into account the possibility that at least in the long run the algorithm will be known by the cryptanalyst. For convenience of exposition we shall take him to be a highly intelligent bad guy; his name shall be Mr. X (see Figure 1.4).

FIGURE 1.4
Mr. X

Imagine that Mr. X has intercepted the following ciphertext.

IOL GYMMUAY XIYM HIN LYGUCH MYWLYN

Based on circumstantial evidence he conjectures that this ciphertext has been encrypted using an additive cipher. (For instance, he could have "found" the machine of Figure 1.3.)

There are two fundamentally different ways to analyze this ciphertext.

1. Exhaustion of all possibilities

Since there are only twenty-six additive ciphers, Mr. X can easily do this. Furthermore, he can reduce the amount of his work considerably if he applies the twenty-six additive ciphers not to the whole text but only to a small part.

Take for example the "word" **HIN**. If he tries all shifts of this sequence, he sees that among all possible cleartext equivalents, the word **not** is the only one that makes sense. Therefore, it is very likely that the ciphertext was obtained by a shift of six positions to the right. Mr. X verifies this conjecture by deciphering the whole ciphertext: **our message does not remain secret**.

The reason this method works so well is that most sequences of letters do not make any sense in English. Though this observation is an important basis of many cryptanalytic methods, it carries a serious disadvantage: this method cannot (or not feasibly) be automated. For a computer to do the cryptanalysis without human interaction, the computer would have to memorize all (or at least very many) English words. Although this is certainly possible, it would be like using a cannon to shoot sparrows. The same cannot be said of the second method.

2. Statistical Analysis

In English, as in any other natural language, letters of the alphabet do not appear equally often; each letter has its characteristic frequency. These frequencies are listed in Table 1.2 (which includes only proper letters, not spaces, punctuation marks, and so on). This table is taken from [BP82]; to obtain the figures, the authors took passages from newspapers and novels. Their total sample contained 100,362 alphabetic characters. It is remarkable how little the distribution of letters varied from one text to the next. There are, of course, obvious differences: in British spelling z is less frequent than in American because -ise is used instead of -ize. Also, the letters in a math text containing many equations involving the variable x, or in a document on the effect of ozone on the zebras of Zaire, would certainly exhibit slightly different relative frequencies.

The letters fall into natural groups according to their relative frequency. In Table 1.3 the letter **e** stands alone as by far the most popular letter. Grouped together in second place are those letters whose frequency is not too small. In the third group are those letters that have a small but significant frequency, whereas the last group consists of the letters that are for cryptographic purposes insignificant.

What happens if we encipher an English cleartext? Well, the frequency distribution of the letters remains as it was—in the sense that if, for instance, **e** is enciphered by **X**, then **X** will be the most frequent letter. If, on the other hand, **k** is enciphered by **I**, then **I** will have a negligible frequency.

letter	relative frequency (%)	letter	relative frequency (%)
a	8.167	n	6.749
b	1.492	o	7.507
c	2.782	p	1.929
d	4.253	q	0.095
e	12.702	4	5.987
f	2.228	s	6.327
g	2.015	t	9.056
h	6.094	u	2.758
i	6.966	v	0.978
j	0.153	w	2.360
k	0.772	x	0.150
l	4.025	y	1.974
m	2.406	z	0.074

TABLE 1.2
Relative frequencies of the letters of the English language

group	frequency of this group of letters in English text	range of the relative frequencies
e	12.7%	more than 12%
t, a, o, i, n, s, h, r	56.9%	6%–9%
d, l	8.3%	4%
c, u, m, w, f, g, y, p, b	19.9%	1.5%–3%
v, k, j, x, q, z	2.2%	less than 1%

TABLE 1.3
Grouping the letters

In practice, the cryptanalyst Mr. X proceeds as follows. First he counts via a list of little strokes how often the single letters of the ciphertext occur. In the above example he gets:

Letter: A B C D E F G H I J K L M N O P Q R S T U V W X Y Z
Frequency: 1 0 1 0 0 0 2 2 3 0 0 3 4 2 1 0 0 0 0 0 2 0 1 1 6 0

The most frequent letter is **Y**. Hence he may assume in first approximation that **Y** corresponds to the cleartext letter **e**. (Caution: Since everything is based on statistics, nothing is 100% certain! Therefore, Mr. X has to look for additional evidence to support his conjecture.)

If the conjecture were correct, then the ciphertext would be obtained by a shift of six positions to the right. Then the letters P, Q, R, S, T would correspond to the cleartext letters v, w, x, y, z—consecutive series of letters with very low frequency. This confirms Mr. X's conjecture, since the letters P, Q, R, S, T do not occur at all in the ciphertext. Moreover, L, M, N would correspond to r, s, t—letters with relatively high frequency. And indeed, L, M, N occur quite often in our text.

Hence, Mr. X will put aside any further doubts and try to decipher according to his conjecture. He gets a sensible cleartext, and his conjecture is proved.

The second method has an indisputable advantage in that a computer may perform it without human interaction. On the other hand, since this method is based on statistics, it requires a little caution. A naive search using only the most frequent letters may, particularly with short texts, lead to incorrect results. But it is possible to design algorithms that work with short texts by making use of more of the available data. In any case, my experience is that while engaged in cryptanalysis I started to believe in statistics!

1.3 MONOALPHABETIC CIPHERS

A cipher is called *monoalphabetic* if any letter of the alphabet is always enciphered by the same (ciphertext) letter. We can describe a monoalphabetic cipher by writing a *ciphertext alphabet* beneath a *cleartext alphabet*. For example, the following systems represent monoalphabetic ciphers:

Cleartext: a b c d e f g h i j k l m n o p q r s t u v w x y z
Ciphertext: Q W E R T Y U I O P A S D F G H J K L Z X C V B N M

Cleartext: a b c d e f g h i j k l m n o p q r s t u v w x y z
Ciphertext: ℵ ∞ ℂ ∂ ⊗ ~ ≈ ℏ ↓ | | ‖ ∠ ℕ ← ↑ · ℝ ∫ ⊥ → ∇ ⊕ × ± √

The last $\otimes \times \aleph \angle \uparrow \| \otimes$ is to remind the reader that cleartext and cipher-text need not be defined over the same alphabet. When the same alphabet is used, then any monoalphabetic cipher corresponds to a permutation of the letters of the alphabet. Conversely, we may attach to any permutation of the letters a monoalphabetic cipher. Hence, we deduce that there are exactly

$$26! = 26 \cdot 25 \cdots 2 \cdot 1 = 403{,}291{,}461{,}126{,}605{,}635{,}584{,}000{,}000 \approx 4 \cdot 10^{26}$$

monoalphabetic ciphers over the natural alphabet $\{a, b, \ldots, z\}$.

In this chapter we study quite a large sample of monoalphabetic ciphers. After considering some examples, we find that monoalphabetic ciphers are not nearly so secure as their impressive abundance might seem to imply.

1.4 AFFINE CIPHERS

When we use a computer for enciphering, usually we identify **a** (and **A**) with 1, **b** (and **B**) with 2, ..., **x** with 24, **y** with 25, and **z** with 0. Using this transcription rule, one can describe additive ciphers particularly well. A shift of s positions to the right, for example, corresponds to the addition of the number s (mod 26), as follows.

- First the cleartext letter is translated ("encoded") into its corresponding number.
- Then s is added to this number.
- Finally, if this sum exceeds 25, the remainder of the sum when divided by 26 is translated back into a letter. (A mathematician would say that one computes modulo 26, or, more briefly, mod 26.)

In such a way one gets the corresponding ciphertext letter.

Example.   We want to encipher the cleartext letter **a** by the additive cipher that is defined by a shift of three positions.

- **a** is translated into 1.
- $1 + 3 = 4$.
- 4 represents the ciphertext letter **D**.

Enciphering **x** works as follows.

- **x** corresponds to 24.
- $24 + 3 = 27$.
- The remainder of 27 when divided by 26 is 1.
- This remainder corresponds to the ciphertext letter **A**.

This method can be understood as *adding* letters. What about *multiplying*? That can be done as follows.

In order to multiply a letter by a number t, we calculate again modulo 26. In other words, we multiply the number which corresponds to the letter by t and use the remainder of this product when divided by 26. This remainder corresponds to a letter, which is the result of the multiplication.

For instance, if we multiply the corresponding value of each cleartext letter by 2, we get the following "ciphertext."

Cleartext: a b c d e f g h i j k l m n o p q r s t u v w x y z
Ciphertext: B D F H J L N P R T V X Z B D F H J L N P R T V X Z

Notice that every product (for instance, **P**) is obtained by two letters (in our example, by **h** and **u**). Therefore, we cannot use this substitution as a cipher—any cipher must satisfy the condition that it *must be possible to reconstruct the cleartext* uniquely *from the ciphertext*. (Some think that this rule is too restrictive. So let us weaken the rule while at the same time giving it credence: *It must be possible for* a computer *to decipher any ciphertext*). Let's take another chance and multiply the letters by 3.

Cleartext: a b c d e f g h i j k l m n o p q r s t u v w x y z
Ciphertext: C F I L O R U X A D G J M P S V Y B E H K N Q T W Z

In this case we actually obtain a monoalphabetic cipher. It can be verified without great effort that one obtains a monoalphabetic cipher when one multiplies by 1, 3, 5, 7, 9, 11, 15, 17, 19, 21, 23, or 25 (see exercise 17). We call the ciphers obtained in this way *multiplicative*.

There are in total just twelve multiplicative ciphers—including the trivial one. This number is even less than the number of additive ciphers. Therefore we expect very limited cryptographic security.

We can, however, combine additive and multiplicative ciphers. In order to do so, we first add the cleartext letter to a number s, interpret the result as an intermediate cleartext letter, and multiply this with a further number t. By this rule we obtain a new cipher which is denoted by $[s, t]$ and called an *affine* cipher (see exercise 7).

The *key* of the affine cipher $[s, t]$ consists of the pair of numbers s and t. (Of course, one must choose the number t in such a way that one gets a multiplicative cipher. So, t is one of the aforementioned numbers 1, 3, 5, 7, 9, 11, 15, 17, 19, 21, 23, or 25.)

The number of all affine ciphers is easily computed as the number of all additive ciphers times the number of all multiplicative ciphers. Therefore, there are $26 \cdot 16 = 312$ affine ciphers. This number is sufficiently large— enough for one a day if you don't send messages on Sundays or holidays— that a naive cryptanalysis without ingenuity leads into trouble. Here we shall not give a specific algorithm for analyzing affine ciphers (but see exercises 14, 15, and 16), since in section 1.6 we will analyze all monoalphabetic ciphers.

1.5 KEYWORDS

By the following method we obtain an extremely large set of monoalphabetic ciphers. For the key we need two ingredients, a *keyword* and a *key letter*. From the keyword we obtain a sequence of distinct letters. This is done by omitting any subsequent appearance of any letter of the chosen word. If, for instance, we choose as our keyword

CRYPTANALYSIS,

then our sequence of letters will be

CRYPTANLSI.

Now we write this sequence of letters beneath the cleartext alphabet in such a way that we start precisely beneath the key letter. If, in our example, the key letter is e, then we obtain

Cleartext: a b c d e f g h i j k l m n o p q r s t u v w x y z
Ciphertext: C R Y P T A N L S

Finally we write the remaining letters in alphabetical order after the last keyword letter. In our example we obtain as the encipherment rule.

Cleartext: a b c d e f g h i j k l m n o p q r s t u v w x y z
Ciphertext: V W X Z C R Y P T A N L S I B D E F G H J K M O Q U

Since we cannot say precisely how many keywords there are, we cannot give the exact number of keyword ciphers, but it is clear that its number is truly enormous. Formally speaking, we get all possible monoalphabetic ciphers—though then we have to allow extremely strange keywords.

1.6 CRYPTANALYSIS

The philosophy of modern cryptanalysis is embodied in Kerckhoffs' principle, as formulated in the book *La cryptographie militaire* (1883) by the Dutch philologist Jean Guillaume Hubert Victor François Alexandre Auguste Kerckhoffs von Nieuwenhof (1835–1903).

Kerckhoffs' Principle.   *The security of a cryptosystem must not depend on keeping secret the crypto algorithm. The security depends only on keeping secret the key.*

This is basically a warning to the designer of systems, who must not bet too heavily that the algorithm will never be known to our Mr. X. There are many instances in history where the inventor of a system based his faith in it on the fact that the algorithm was not known to the cryptanalyst. On the contrary, the task is to design a system which remains secure even if the algorithm becomes completely public. A famous example is the publication of the Data Encryption Standard (DES; see Exercise 22).

The cryptanalyst works under varying circumstances that make his task more or less difficult; for example, the following types of attack may be differentiated.

Known ciphertext attack. The cryptanalyst knows a rather long part of a ciphertext. This is a reasonable supposition since it is often not difficult to obtain arbitrarily long parts of a ciphertext.

Known plaintext attack. The cryptanalyst knows a relatively small part of plaintext and corresponding ciphertext. Such a scenario is more realistic than it may seem at first glance, for the cryptanalyst often has some idea of the content of a message and can guess some critical words. For instance, most people cannot resist using standard set phrases at the beginning and the end of a letter.

Chosen plaintext attack. If the cryptanalyst has access to the algorithm (with the actual key!), then he can feed in specially chosen messages (for instance very regular ones, such as a sequence consisting of only one letter: **aaaaa**...) in order to obtain information about the key. How dangerous such an attack is becomes clear when we realize that some crypto devices cannot only encipher but also "sign" messages (see chapter 5). If an algorithm is so weak that it allows a chosen plaintext attack, then Mr. X can produce out of signed messages that seem to be completely innocent a document that has a valid signature—and that can do great damage to the original sender.

Every monoalphabetic cipher of a natural language can be broken rather easily. I shall convince the reader of this under the extremely weak (and realistic) assumption of a known ciphertext. I shall, however, present only the outline of a method. Its aim is to convince the reader that monoalphabetic ciphers are extremely insecure. The algorithm relies on the fact that the nine _ost _re__ent _etters o_ an en__ish te_t _ro_i_e _ore than t_o thir_s o_ the entire te_t.

Imagine that Mr. X has intercepted a ciphertext consisting of approximately 500 letters. Assume that he knows (or conjectures) that this ciphertext was produced using a monoalphabetic cipher.

Step 1. By counting the frequencies of the letters in the ciphertext, he identifies the ciphertext equivalent of **e** and also the ciphertext equivalents of the letters in the second group, namely t, a, o, i, n, s, h, r—but only as a set, not as identifiable letters.

The next task is to identify some of these letters. For this purpose, knowledge of the single-letter statistics is not sufficient.

Step 2. In English, as in any other language, pairs of consecutive letters (called *bigrams*) occur with distinct frequencies. What is the most frequent bigram? Well, the most frequent *trigram* (sequence of three consecutive letters) is the word *the*. From this it should be plausible that *he* is the most frequent bigram.

What can Mr. X deduce from these observations? Well, for all the letters in the second group exactly one, namely **h**, has a very high frequency when combined with the already identified letter **e**. Thus, he has identified **h**. Counting the trigrams consisting of a letter in the second group and **he**, he is also able to identify **t**. Also, apart from **the**, there is only one other trigram of the above form with noteworthy frequency, namely **she**.

Thus, Mr. X knows the ciphertext equivalents of the letters e, t, h, s, which make up more than one-third of the text! With care he can identify in this direct way a few other letters (see exercise 21).

Step 3. Now he lets a computer translate the letters already identified. In other words, the computer deciphers the known parts of the text. This will be displayed at the terminal, where the undeciphered letters are shown as blanks.

Usually the text is not yet intelligible. But it is easy for the intelligent Mr. X to guess further letters. Then the text—using the additional identifications—will again be shown on the screen. After repeating the process a couple of times Mr. X will arrive at a reasonably intelligible text.

In sum, monoalphabetic ciphers over natural languages are remarkably insecure. (A natural language has few letters that are distributed nonuniformly.) Today, therefore, people either use monoalphabetic ciphers over *nonnatural languages*, or they advance to *poly*alphabetic ciphers.

The most popular monoalphabetic cipher is the DES, the Data Encryption Standard. This algorithm was essentially developed by IBM. (For a brief history see [DP89].) The DES enciphers not letters but the bits 0 and 1, or, more precisely, 64 bits per stroke. (Clearly, if the DES is used to encipher an ordinary text, the letters first must be coded with bits; one method to do this, the ASCII code, will be explained in chapter 5.) It turns out that the DES is a monoalphabetic cipher over the alphabet $\{(a_1, \ldots, a_{64}) \mid a_i \in \{0, 1\}\}$. Thus, the elements of the plaintext and ciphertext alphabets are all binary sequences of length 64. For the key one can choose any sequence of 56 bits.

This was the first algorithm in history to be made public in all its details right from the beginning. Part of the official description of the DES is quoted in exercise 22. (The entire document is reprinted in [BP82].) The DES is widely and successfully used, particularly in banking. More or less regularly occurring rumors that the DES has been broken have never been substantiated. In any case, attacks have not damaged its popularity. On the contrary, in 1990 Biham and Shamir [BS93] presented a sophisticated attack on the DES, and one of their insights was that the DES was designed using excellent criteria: given the short key length, it is a very good algorithm. Most experts had been convinced that longer keys were better. Another result of the work of Biham and Shamir was that many DES-like algorithms were broken. Perhaps this shows better than anything else that the art of designing a good algorithm is not widely understood.

EXERCISES

1. What is the message corresponding to the following ciphertext, which was obtained using a scytale?

   L G O A B I A I R F R E N P K E H S E G H E A I E N I I M T S E
   S N C A G T M A C S N E O S D R U Y N R T L Y B O E Y O Y P
   T F R C H L T L T A A A A O E H L E V C G T E S S E K R Y.

2. Build yourself a scytale. (Note that instead of a cylinder, you may also use a flat, stiff piece of paper. In this case, when enciphering, you must be careful not to fold the ribbon.)
   (a) Try the cipher above.
   (b) Describe this cipher using the notions of algorithm and key.
   (c) What is, approximately, the number of keys?
   (d) Is this a secure cipher?

3. The "rail-fence cipher" is best explained by an example.

   Cleartext: I   I   O   I   R
             S H S G O C P E ?
               T   A   D   H
   Ciphertext: **I I O I R S H S G O C P E ? T A D H**
   (a) Describe this cipher.
   (b) Is this a transposition cipher or a substitution cipher?

4. And Caesar said **SBKF SFAF SFZF**.

5. Construct a working model of the machine of Figure 1.3. (A poor man's version of such a machine can be constructed by writing the alphabet *twice* across the top of a page and *once*, using the same spacing, across the top of a second page.)

6. Why are additive ciphers called *additive*?

▷ 7. Look up what affine geometry is (see, for example, Coxeter, *Introduction to Geometry* [Cox69]) and explain why affine ciphers are called *affine*.

@ 8. Write a computer program which realizes a monoalphabetic cipher. Your program should have the cleartext and the key as input; it should be possible for the user to choose the key.

9. Search for proper English words that can be obtained from one another using an additive cipher.

10. Count the letter frequencies of five samples having 1000 letters each from a variety of sources.

11. Compose a cleartext with at least 50 letters in which *e* is not the most frequent letter. (Hint: This task is much too difficult for an author such as I, but it is probably a snap for you.)

Additional information.   A text in which a particular letter is deliberately avoided merits, believe it or not, the scholarly label *lipogram*. The earliest lipogrammatic writer is said to have been Lasus of Achaia, a Greek poet of the 6th century B.C. There are examples of lipogrammatic writing throughout history, but the most remarkable has to be the 1969 French novel *La Disparition* by George Perec—none of its more than 85,000 words contains the letter *e*. Such a feat should give the cryptanalyst pause, if not a nightmare. More on this unusual literary tradition may be obtained from the second edition of the *Oxford English Dictionary*.

12. Count the bigrams in at least two samples having 1000 letters each.

@ 13. Write a program that counts the frequencies of the letters of a given text.

@ 14. Construct an algorithm that breaks a ciphertext of thirty letters that was obtained by an additive cipher. The algorithm should use as its main ingredient only the frequencies of the letters.

15. (a) Decipher **GDZKXG**, assuming an affine cipher $[5, t]$ was used and that the cleartext is a name.

   (b) Decipher **SXWGR**, assuming an affine cipher $[s, 3]$ was used and that the cleartext is a name.

16. (a) Show that every multiplicative cipher maps **m** onto **M** and **z** onto **Z**.

   (b) By how many corresponding pairs of cleartext and ciphertext letters is an affine cipher determined?

@ 17. Using the results of the preceding exercise, write a program which breaks an affine cipher under a known plaintext attack.

18. (a) Prove that a multiplication of the letters of an alphabet by a number t produces a cipher if and only if t and 26 are *relatively prime* (that is, if the greatest common divisor of t and 26 is 1).

   (b) How many multiplicative ciphers does an alphabet of twenty-five, of twenty-seven, or of twenty-nine letters have?

@ 19. Design an algorithm which enciphers using a keyword and a key letter. The program should have the property that the keyword and the keyletter can be chosen by the user.

▷ 20. Decipher the following text. You may assume that a keyword cipher with an English keyword was used.

HEXFX CG ICHHIX WAJQH HEPH HEX BFAQIXT AZ
BFAHXVHCYS PYW GXVJFCYS VATTJYCVPHCAYG LCII
VAYHCYJX HA SFAL WJFCYS HEX VATCYS NXPFG YAH
AYIN CY CHG HFPWCHCAYPI TCICHPFN PYW BAICHCVPI
FAIXG QJH PIGA CY HEX BJQICV PYW VATTXFVCPI
WATPCYG.

(Hint: This is not an easy exercise. Look at the three-letter words and note that the most frequent three-letter words in English are *the* and *and*. Furthermore, look at the last three letters of the words and take into account that the most frequent three-letter ending is *ing*.)

21. (a) By reasoning and later verifying, discover some frequent and infrequent bigrams and trigrams in English. (You may also consult Appendix 1 of [BP82].)

   (b) Based on these facts, try to improve Step 2 of our proposed cryptanalysis of a monoalphabetic cipher.

22. Read carefully the following official document concerning the standardization of the DES algorithm. Convince yourself that the general statements are true. Where is Kerckhoffs' principle expressed?

**Federal Information
Processing Standards Publication 46**
1977 January 15
ANNOUNCING THE
DATA ENCRYPTION STANDARD

Name of Standard. Data Encryption Standard (DES).

Category of Standard. Operations, Computer Security.

Explanation. The Data Encryption Standard (DES) specifies an algorithm to be implemented in electronic hardware devices and used for the cryptographic protection of computer data. This publication provides a complete description of a mathematical algorithm for encrypting (enciphering) and decrypting (deciphering) binary coded information. Encrypting data converts it to an unintelligible form called cipher. Decrypting cipher converts the data back to its original form. The algorithm described in this standard specifies both enciphering and deciphering operations which are based on a binary number called a key. The key consists of 64 binary digits ('0's or '1's) of which 56 bits are used directly by the algorithm and 8 bits are used for error detection.

Binary coded data may be cryptographically protected using the DES algorithm in conjunction with a key. Each member of a group of authorized users of encrypted computer data must have the key that was used to encipher the data in order to use it. This key, held by each member in common, is used to decipher the data received in cipher form from other members of the group. The encryption algorithm specified in this standard is commonly known among those using the standard. The unique key chosen for use in a particular application makes the results of encrypting data using the algorithm unique. Selection of a different key causes the cipher that is produced for any given set of inputs to be different. The cryptographic security of the data depends on the security provided for the key used to encipher and decipher the data.

Data can be recovered from cipher only by using exactly the same key used to encipher it. Unauthorized recipients of the cipher who know the algorithm but do not have the correct key cannot derive the original data algorithmically. However, anyone who does have the key and the algorithm can easily decipher the cipher and obtain the original data. A standard algorithm based on a secure key thus provides a basis for exchanging encrypted computer data by issuing the key used to encipher it to those authorized to have the data.

Applications. Data encryption (cryptography) may be utilized in various applications and in various environments. In general, cryptography is used to protect data while it is being communicated between two points or while it is stored in a medium vulnerable to physical theft. Communication security provides protection to data by enciphering it at the transmitting point and deciphering it at the receiving point. File security provides protection to data by enciphering it when it is recorded on a storage medium and deciphering it when it is read back from the storage medium. In the first case, the key must be available at the transmitter and receiver simultaneously during communication. In the second case, the key must be maintained and accessible for the duration of the storage period.

Qualifications. The cryptographic algorithm specified in this standard transforms a 64-bit binary value into a unique 64-bit binary value based on a 56-bit variable. If the complete 64-bit input is used (i.e., none of the input bits should be predetermined from block to block) and if the 56-bit variable is randomly chosen, no technique other than trying all possible keys using known input and output for the DES will guarantee finding the chosen key. As there are over 70,000,000,000,000,000 (seventy quadrillion) possible keys of 56 bits, the feasibility of deriving a particular key in this way is extremely unlikely in typical threat environments. Moreover, if the key is changed frequently, the risk of this event is greatly diminished. However, users should be aware that it is theoretically possible to derive the key in fewer trials (with a correspondingly lower probability of success depending on the number of keys tried) and should be cautioned to change the key as often as practical. Users must change the key and provide it a high level of protection in order to minimize the potential risks of its unauthorized computation or acquisition.

When correctly implemented and properly used, this standard will provide a high level of cryptographic protection to computer data.

23. Many ciphers that are popular among children (and others) work in such a way that all letters remain *as* they are but not *where* they are: they are rearranged in more or less strange patterns.

    For the next cipher, sender and recipient have to have identical templates, consisting of many square holes cut from a rectangle. The sender places the template onto a piece of paper and writes his message through the holes, in natural order, one letter per hole. Then he removes the template and fills up the blank positions with arbitrary letters. If the message exceeds the number of holes then he has to use the template several times. The encrypted message is sent to the recipient, who can read it easily by blocking out the nonsense letters with his template (see Figure 1.5).

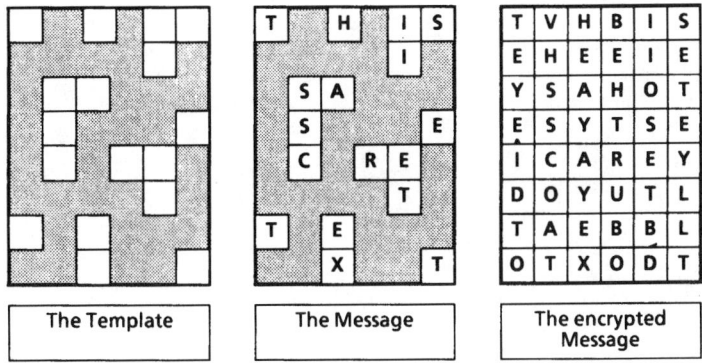

| The Template | The Message | The encrypted Message |

FIGURE 1.5

A paper-and-pencil cipher

(a) Try the cipher. (Hint: As letters for camouflage I use the letters of "ordinary" sentences, but distribute them randomly on the paper. So the letters are distributed as in normal English texts.)

(b) Would you count this cipher among the transposition ciphers or among the substitution ciphers?

(c) What are the keys? How many keys are there (approximately)?

(d) Under what circumstances does a cryptanalyst have a chance at deciphering such a message?

(e) What is the content of the following cryptogram?

H	K	A	C	P	P
T	E	B	M	Y	O
U	B	I	H	F	O
R	R	T	S	E	H
E	H	V	E	A	D
L	U	E	A	Y	L
T	A	O	S	M	R
H	E	Y	C	O	U

Chapter 2

WORDS AND WORMS
or
WHY DO IT IN A SIMPLE WAY, IF YOU CAN DO IT IN A COMPLICATED WAY?

> A word, a phrase: From ciphers arise
> perceived life, a flash of meaning.
>
> —Gottfried Benn

In this chapter we deal with polyalphabetic ciphers. With this kind of cipher a given cleartext letter will not always be enciphered into the same ciphertext letter. As a consequence, a polyalphabetic cipher cannot simply be described by a cleartext alphabet with a ciphertext alphabet underneath.

On the other hand, enciphering cannot be performed arbitrarily, otherwise a recipient is no better off than a cryptanalyst. Thus, deciphering should be unique—and, of course, as simple as possible. Typically enciphering is unique as well, but not necessarily. Enciphering is not unique in a *homophonic* cipher, for example, as explained in the first example of this chapter. In the central part of the chapter I will deal with those polyalphabetic algorithms that are a combination of different monoalphabetic ciphers; the Vigenère cipher is a typical example.

2.1 EQUALIZING THE FREQUENCIES

How can the frequencies of ciphertext symbols be made equal? Simply enough: Use an enciphering rule that assigns to any cleartext letter not just one ciphertext symbol, but a whole *set* of ciphertext symbols according to the following conditions:

- In order to make deciphering unique, the sets belonging to distinct cleartext letters must be disjoint.
- The number of ciphertext symbols assigned to a cleartext letter is determined by the frequency of that letter. (Here we use the relative frequency from Table 1.2 suitably rounded.)

In our example the ciphertext symbols are the 100 pairs of digits $00, \ldots, 99$, assigned according to Table 2.1.

a:	05, 18, 26, 38, 45, 54, 62, 84
b:	10
c:	28, 06, 80
d:	24, 46, 85, 88
e:	15, 16, 23, 31, 44, 61, 69, 77, 83, 87, 91, 95
f:	02, 32
g:	17, 52
h:	03, 09, 33, 76, 82, 89
i:	27, 47, 66, 73, 74, 81, 90
j:	11
k:	43
l:	19, 37, 48, 68
m:	00, 35
n:	20, 36, 53, 65, 97, 98
o:	22, 30, 34, 60, 64, 67, 72
p:	04, 39
q:	59
r:	08, 56, 57, 71, 79, 92
s:	21, 42, 49, 63, 70, 94
t:	12, 50, 51, 55, 75, 78, 86, 93, 96, 99
u:	29, 01, 58
v:	14
w:	13, 25
x:	41
y:	40
z:	07

TABLE 2.1
A homophonic cipher

When a cleartext is *enciphered*, the sender randomly chooses for any cleartext letter one of the corresponding symbols. By using the above table, deciphering is easy: 66 887246 208050 1209736543 86333899 7455 8170 4230 15454940.

Since the ciphertext representative of a given letter is chosen randomly, any symbol (in our example, any pair of digits) occurs with the same probability, hence the name *homophonic*. A potential cryptanalyst is confronted with a much more difficult task than breaking a monoalphabetic cipher.

But the designer of such a system should not celebrate too soon, since cryptanalysis is, of course, possible. The analysis is based on the observation that although the frequencies of the single ciphertext symbols are equal, one can deduce information about the nature of the symbols by observing *pairs* of symbols (see Step 2 of section 1.6). I won't go deeply into detail, but will give an example.

If one considers a ciphertext symbol corresponding to the cleartext letter **t**, for instance, then one observes that certain symbols come after it with a high probability; these symbols correspond to the cleartext letter **h**.

Of course, this only hints at how to design a cryptanalysis. The aim is to suggest to the reader that a clever cryptanalyst may also analyze a ciphertext that, at first glance, seems unbreakable.

2.2 THE VIGENÈRE CIPHER

The Vigenère cipher was published in 1586 by the French diplomat Blaise de Vigenère (1523–1596). The basic idea of this cipher was to use a number of monoalphabetic ciphers in turn. Since the idea is so natural, Vigenère ciphers have been reinvented more than once—of course, in slightly different forms. Two of the important predecessors are Johannes Trithemius (1462–1516), whose books *Poligraphia* (1518) and *Stegonographia* (1531) were published posthumously, and Giovanni Battista Della Porta (1535–1615), better known as the inventor of the camera obscura. In 1558, in his book *Magia Naturalis*, Della Porta published a polyalphabetic cipher quite similar to Vigenère's system.

In this chapter I shall focus on the Vigenère cipher, the most popular among the periodic polyalphabetic ciphers for a twofold reason:

- It served as a prototype for many ciphers that have been used by professionals, even in our century.

- In breaking the Vigenère cipher the reader shall learn two important methods, the Kasiski test and the Friedman test.

In order to work with the Vigenère cipher one needs two things: a *keyword* and the *Vigenère square* (see Figure 2.1).

This square consists of twenty-six copies of the alphabet arranged in such a way that the first is the usual alphabet, the second is the usual alphabet shifted by one position, the third is shifted by two positions, and so forth. In other words, the Vigenère square consists of all 26 additive ciphers in natural order.

```
Cleartext:   a b c d e f g h i j k l m n o p q r s t u v w x y z

             A B C D E F G H I J K L M N O P Q R S T U V W X Y Z
             B C D E F G H I J K L M N O P Q R S T U V W X Y Z A
             C D E F G H I J K L M N O P Q R S T U V W X Y Z A B
             D E F G H I J K L M N O P Q R S T U V W X Y Z A B C
             E F G H I J K L M N O P Q R S T U V W X Y Z A B C D
             F G H I J K L M N O P Q R S T U V W X Y Z A B C D E
             G H I J K L M N O P Q R S T U V W X Y Z A B C D E F
             H I J K L M N O P Q R S T U V W X Y Z A B C D E F G
             I J K L M N O P Q R S T U V W X Y Z A B C D E F G H
             J K L M N O P Q R S T U V W X Y Z A B C D E F G H I
             K L M N O P Q R S T U V W X Y Z A B C D E F G H I J
             L M N O P Q R S T U V W X Y Z A B C D E F G H I J K
             M N O P Q R S T U V W X Y Z A B C D E F G H I J K L
             N O P Q R S T U V W X Y Z A B C D E F G H I J K L M
             O P Q R S T U V W X Y Z A B C D E F G H I J K L M N
             P Q R S T U V W X Y Z A B C D E F G H I J K L M N O
             Q R S T U V W X Y Z A B C D E F G H I J K L M N O P
             R S T U V W X Y Z A B C D E F G H I J K L M N O P Q
             S T U V W X Y Z A B C D E F G H I J K L M N O P Q R
             T U V W X Y Z A B C D E F G H I J K L M N O P Q R S
             U V W X Y Z A B C D E F G H I J K L M N O P Q R S T
             V W X Y Z A B C D E F G H I J K L M N O P Q R S T U
             W X Y Z A B C D E F G H I J K L M N O P Q R S T U V
             X Y Z A B C D E F G H I J K L M N O P Q R S T U V W
             Y Z A B C D E F G H I J K L M N O P Q R S T U V W X
             Z A B C D E F G H I J K L M N O P Q R S T U V W X Y
```

FIGURE 2.1
The Vigenère square

The keyword may be any sequence of letters; by way of example we choose the word VENUS. We write this keyword repeatedly, letter by letter, above the cleartext (without spaces) until reaching the end of the cleartext:

Keyword: V E N U S V E N U S V E N U
Cleartext: p o l y a l p h a b e t i c

The enciphering rule is as follows: The letter of the keyword that is above a certain cleartext letter determines the alphabet (that is, the *row* of the Vigenère square) that will be used to encipher this cleartext letter.

For instance: In order to obtain the first ciphertext letter, we go to the *row* beginning with V and take the entry in *column* **p**—this is the letter **K**.

Do you want another example? Here it is: In order to encipher the second letter, we look in row E at the entry in column o, which is **S**.

Continuing in this fashion, we get, finally:

Keyword: V E N U S V E N U S V E N U
Cleartext: p o l y a l p h a b e t i c
Ciphertext: **K S Y S S G T U U T Z X V W**

Clearly, breaking such a cipher provides a greater challenge for Mr. X than analyzing a monoalphabetic cipher. One reason for this is that the ciphertext letters tend to be rather equally distributed. This is suggested even by our small example: The repeated cleartext letter **a** is enciphered into distinct ciphertext letters, namely **S** and **U**. On the other hand, the same ciphertext letter **S** comes from distinct cleartext letters o, y, and **a**.

2.3 CRYPTANALYSIS

Of course, using today's methods, one can analyze a ciphertext obtained by a Vigenère cipher. A ciphertext that is long enough has many regularities; those regularities can be extracted from the text by statistical methods, making it possible to obtain the key word. The first published successful attack on the Vigenère cipher was undertaken in 1863 by the Prussian colonel Friedrich Wilhelm Kasiski (1805–1881). A second method is due to his American counterpart William Frederick Friedman (1891–1969). Both methods aim at determining the length of the keyword. Since they also have fundamental importance for cryptanalysis in general, I shall present them in detail.

```
D B Z M G    A O I Y S    O P V F H    O W K B W
X Z P J L    V V R F G    N B K I X    D V U I M
O P F Q L    V V P U D    K P R V W    O A R L W
D V L M W    A W I N Z    D A K B W    M M R L W
Q I I C G    P A K Y U    C V Z K M    Z A R P S

D T R V D    Z W E Y G    A B Y Y E    Y M G Y F
Y A F H L    C M W L W    L C V H L    M M G Y L
D B Z I F    J N C Y L    O M I A J    J C G M A
I B V R L    O P V F W    O B V L K    O P V U J
Z D V L Q    X W D G G    I Q E Y F    B T Z M Z

D V R M M    A N Z W A    Z V K F Q    G W E A L
Z F K N Z    Z Z V C K    V D V L Q    B W F X U
C I E W W    O P R M U    J Z I Y K    K W E X A
I O I Y H    Z I K Y V    G M K N W    M O I I M
K A D U Q    W M W I M    I L Z H L    C M T C H

C M I N W    S B R H V    O P V S O    D T C M G
H M K C E    Z A S Y D    J K R N W    Y I K C F
O M I P S    G A F Z K    J U V G M    G B Z J D
Z W W N Z    Z V L G T    Z Z F Z S    G X Y U T
Z B J C F    P A V N Z    Z A V W S    I J V Z G

P V U V Q    N K R H F    D V X N Z    Z K Z J Z
Z Z K Y P    O I E X X    M W D N Z    Z Q I M H
V K Z H Y    D V K Y D    G Q X Y F    O O L Y K
N M J G S    Y M R M L    J B Y Y F    P U S Y J
J N R F H    C I S Y L    N
```

FIGURE 2.2
A ciphertext

Suppose that Mr. X has intercepted the ciphertext in Figure 2.2, and suppose that there is reason to believe that this text was produced by a Vigenère cipher. The Kasiski and Friedman tests will allow us to learn things about the keyword.

The Kasiski Test. Although this powerful method of analyzing poly-alphabetic ciphers was first *published* by Kasiski, it should be noted that the English mathematician Charles Babbage (1792–1871)—famous for his pioneering conception of a forerunner to the modern computer—did extensive (though unpublished) work on cryptology. In particular, he devised the Kasiski method in 1854, nine years before Kasiski's work was published. For a detailed account, the reader is referred to [Fra84].

The basic idea is as follows. If the cleartext repeats sequences of letters (for example, the word **the**) then, in general, the corresponding ciphertext sequences are distinct. Indeed, even the first cleartext letter of the two sequences will usually be enciphered differently. If, however, the first letter of a repeated sequence is enciphered by the same keyword letter, then of course the corresponding leading letters of the ciphertexts will be equal. In this situation, also the subsequent letters of the sequence will be enciphered using the same keyword letters; therefore the sequence of letters in corresponding ciphertexts will be repeated. In other words: If the first letters of repeated cleartext sequences are enciphered by the same keyword letter, then the corresponding ciphertext sequences consist of the same letters.

But when does it happen that two cleartext letters are enciphered using the same keyword letter? Well, this happens if the keyword fits between these two letters exactly once, or twice, or three times, or . . . . In other words, if the distance between the two cleartext letters under consideration is a multiple of the length of the keyword (see Figure 2.3).

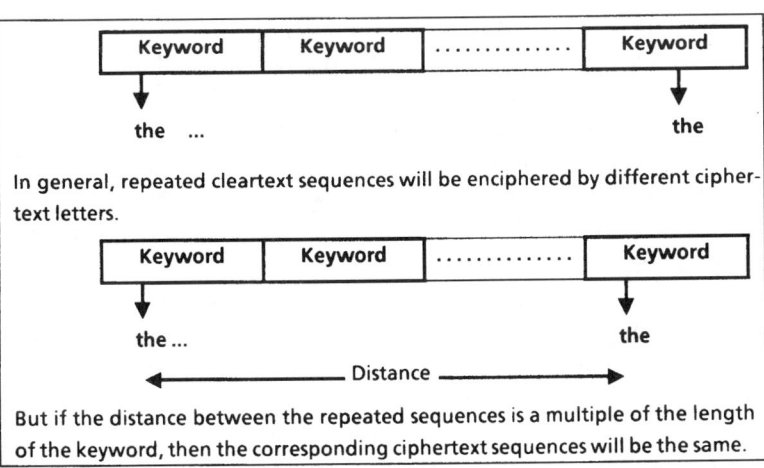

FIGURE 2.3
The Kasiski test

To sum up: If a cleartext sequence is repeated at a distance that is a multiple of the length of the keyword, then the corresponding ciphertext sequences are also repeated.

The cryptanalyst turns the tables. If Mr. X finds repeated sequences in the ciphertext, then he guesses that the distance between these two sequences is most probably a multiple of the length of the keyword. This probability obeys the rule: "the longer the better." We know that equal single letters in the ciphertext give no information at all about the length of the keyword. Also, equal pairs can occur accidentally. But equal sequences consisting of three or more letters are a rather effective tool in discovering the length of the keyword.

Figure 2.4 shows the result of a search for repeated sequences of three or more letters in our ciphertext. The greatest common divisor of the distances is 5, as illustrated in Table 2.2. So, an optimistic cryptanalyst might declare, "Therefore I know that the length of the keyword is 5." (Indeed, in practice the Kasiski test works very well.) The cryptanalyst Mr. X, however, is cautious and says only, "There is a strong indication that the length of the keyword is 5." Why should he be cautious? There are two reasons to be careful.

- It might be the case that, accidentally, two ciphertext sequences with equal letters occur whose distance is not divisible by 5. In such a situation, a naive computation would yield greatest common divisor equal to 1. (In our example, this situation occurs; the sequence **Z Z K** occurs twice—with distance 6.) This means that one should not allow a mindless machine to compute the length of the keyword, but one should do it sensibly. For instance, after computing the greatest common denominators between pairs of distances, one can isolate (and ignore) suspect distances.
- It is conceivable that the length of the keyword is not 5, but rather 10, 15, ... In other words, the Kasiski test gives the length of the keyword only *up to a multiple* (or a *divisor*).

For such reasons (but not only for such reasons) we present another method, which gives the *order of magnitude* of the length of the keyword. The combination of these methods will, most likely, considerably restrict the number of possible key lengths.

```
D B Z M G    A O I Y S    O P V F H    O W K B W
X Z P J L    V V R F G    N B K I X    D V U I M
O P F Q L    V V P U D    K P R V W    O A R L W
D V L M W    A W I N Z    D A K B W    M M R L W
Q I I C G    P A K Y U    C V Z K M    Z A R P S

D T R V D    Z W E Y G    A B Y Y E    Y M G Y F
Y A F H L    C M W L W    L C V H L    M M G Y L
D B Z I F    J N C Y L    O M I A J    J C G M A
I B V R L    O P V F W    O B V L K    O P V U J
Z D V L Q    X W D G G    I Q E Y F    B T Z M Z

D V R M M    A N Z W A    Z V K F Q    G W E A L
Z F K N Z    Z Z V C K    V D V L Q    B W F X U
C I E W W    O P R M U    J Z I Y K    K W E X A
I O I Y H    Z I K Y V    G M K N W    M O I I M
K A D U Q    W M W I M    I L Z H L    C M T C H

C M I N W    S B R H V    O P V S O    D T C M G
H M K C E    Z A S Y D    J K R N W    Y I K C F
O M I P S    G A F Z K    J U V G M    G B Z J D
Z W W N Z    Z V L G T    Z Z F Z S    G X Y U T
Z B J C F    P A V N Z    Z A V W S    I J V Z G

P V U V Q    N K R H F    D V X N ~~Z~~   ~~Z~~~~K~~ Z J Z
~~Z~~~~Z~~~~K~~ Y P    O I E X X    M W D N Z    Z Q I M H
V K Z H Y    D V K Y D    G Q X Y F    O O L Y K
N M J G S    Y M R M L    J B Y Y F    P U S Y J
J N R F H    C I S Y L    N
```

FIGURE 2.4
Sequences consisting of the same letters

Sequence	Distance	Prime factor decomposition of the distance
O P V F	155	$5 \cdot 31$
L V V	20	$2 \cdot 2 \cdot 5$
M G Y	20	$2 \cdot 2 \cdot 5$
D V L Q	50	$2 \cdot 5 \cdot 5$
N Z Z	25, 20	$5 \cdot 5, 2 \cdot 2 \cdot 5$

TABLE 2.2
Evaluation of the sequences consisting of the same letters

The Friedman Test.   This method was invented in 1925 by the renowned American cryptologist Colonel William Frederick Friedman. The apt question for understanding this test is the following: *If one selects a pair of letters from a text, what is the probability that the two letters are equal?* The answer is described by the index of coincidence.

Consider therefore an arbitrary sequence of letters of length n. Let n_1 denote the number of **a**'s, n_2 the number of **b**'s, $\ldots$, n_{26} the number of **z**'s.

We are interested in how often a randomly selected pair of letters would both be **a**. (Note that we do not assume that the pairs under consideration consist of consecutive letters of the text.) Well, for choosing the first letter **a** there are exactly n_1 possibilities; this leaves $n_1 - 1$ possibilities for the second **a**. Since we will neglect the order of the letters in the pair, the number of pairs under consideration equals

$$\frac{n_1(n_1 - 1)}{2}.$$

Therefore, the number of pairs that consist of equal letters (that is either both **a**, or both **b**, $\ldots$, or both **z**) equals

$$\frac{n_1(n_1 - 1)}{2} + \frac{n_2(n_2 - 1)}{2} + \cdots + \frac{n_{26}(n_{26} - 1)}{2} = \sum_{i=1}^{26} \frac{n_i(n_i - 1)}{2}.$$

So, the *chance* of choosing at random a pair of equal letters can be computed to the tune of "number of good cases divided by the number of all cases" as

$$\frac{\sum_{i=1}^{26} n_i(n_i - 1)/2}{n(n - 1)/2} = \frac{\sum_{i=1}^{26} n_i(n_i - 1)}{n(n - 1)}.$$

This number (which is between 0 and 1) is called the *index of coincidence* and is denoted by I:

$$I = \frac{\sum_{i=1}^{26} n_i(n_i - 1)}{n(n - 1)}.$$

Friedman himself denoted it by κ (Greek kappa) and, for this reason, the method is sometimes called the *Kappa test*.

Now we try to compute the index of coincidence in another way. We know that *in natural languages every letter occurs with a characteristic probability*. So, the letter **a** occurs with probability p_1, **b** occurs with probability $p_2, \ldots$, and **z** occurs with probability p_{26}. As an example consider the English language; the probabilities $p_1, p_2, \ldots$ can be found in Table 1.2.

Now think of two arbitrarily chosen letters in our text. The probability that **a** is in the first position is p_1; so, the probability that in *both* positions we will find the letter **a** is (for all practical purposes) $p_1 \cdot p_1$. (The probability is exactly p_1^2 only if one is allowed to choose the same position twice—but when n is large this discrepancy can be ignored.) One reasons similarly for the other letters. Therefore, the probability that in two arbitrarily chosen positions we find the same letter (that is either the letter **a**, or the letter **b**, $\ldots$, or the letter **z**) equals

$$p_1 \cdot p_1 + p_2 \cdot p_2 + \cdots + p_{26} \cdot p_{26} = \sum_{i=1}^{26} p_i^2.$$

Clearly, this number depends on the probabilities $p_1, \ldots, p_{26}$. We compute two examples.

- For the English language one has

$$\sum_{i=1}^{26} p_i^2 \approx 0.065.$$

  This means that if pairs of letters are repeatedly chosen from an English text, then roughly 6.5% of the time the letters of the pair would be the same.

- On the other hand, imagine a purely random text, that is a text in which the letters are completely muddled. Then every letter occurs with the same probability $p_1 = 1/26$. We get in this case

$$\sum_{i=1}^{26} p_i^2 = \sum_{i=1}^{26} \frac{1}{26^2} = 26 \cdot \frac{1}{26^2} = \frac{1}{26} \approx 0.038.$$

So, the chance of finding a pair of equal letters in such a letter salad is only about half as great as in a respectable English document.

Now we turn to cryptology, but not yet to the cryptanalysis of the Vigenère cipher. We first make two important observations.

- If the probabilities $p_1, \ldots, p_{26}$ are known (as they are in English) then the sum of their squares is (approximately) equal to the index of coincidence:

$$I \approx \sum_{i=1}^{26} p_i^2.$$

One can prove that I (or, equivalently, $\sum p_i^2$) becomes *larger* if the text under consideration becomes more *irregular*, and, conversely, that I becomes smaller the more regular the text is. The value .038 is the absolute minimum for an index of coincidence. (This assertion is the subject of exercise 14.)

- Let us go back for a moment to monoalphabetic ciphers. Since a monoalphabetic cipher is simply a permutation of the letters, the probability distribution is the same in the cleartext as in the ciphertext. (The probabilities are permuted together with the letters. For instance, the probability .082 is assigned in the cleartext to the letter **a**, while in the ciphertext to the ciphertext equivalent of **a**.)

　As a consequence, the index of coincidence is invariant under a monoalphabetic cipher. On the other hand, using a polyalphabetic cipher, the index of coincidence decreases; recall that polyalphabetic ciphers were developed in order to equalize the frequencies of the letters. Thus we obtain a *test* that tells us whether or not a given ciphertext was obtained by a monoalphabetic cipher: Compute the index of coincidence of the ciphertext in question. If this index is about .065, then the cipher used is probably monoalphabetic. If, however, the index is significantly smaller than .065, then it is very likely that a polyalphabetic cipher was used.

　Now, at last, we return to the Vigenère cipher, exploiting the index of coincidence in order to obtain information on the length of the keyword. Our aim is to compute, from a theoretical point of view, the index of coincidence of a text that has been enciphered using a Vigenère cipher. Since it is a polyalphabetic cipher it is clear from the preceding observations that the index of coincidence will be smaller than .065. But how much smaller? Answer: It depends. More precisely: It depends in an essential way upon the length l of the keyword.

　This will in turn allow us to determine l from the index of coincidence for a given ciphertext. Developing the formula is a trifle messy, though not really difficult. If you are not in the mood just now for manipulating mathematical formulas, feel free to turn over the next pages and join us at the beginning of the next section.

Let l denote the length of the keyword. For the sake of simplicity we assume that the keyword consists of distinct letters.

Imagine now that the ciphertext had been organized with its letters entered in l columns. Thus in the first column there appear letters in positions number $1, l+1, 2l+1$, and so on—all those letters that have been enciphered using the first letter of the keyword. Similarly, in the second column we find those letters of the ciphertext that have been enciphered using the second letter of the keyword. Figure 2.5 shows this pattern.

Letter S_i of the keyword	S_1	S_2	S_3	$\cdots$	S_p
	1	2	3	$\cdots$	p
	$l+1$	$l+2$	$l+3$	$\cdots$	$2l$
	$2l+1$	$2l+2$	$\cdots$		$3l$
	$3l+1$	$\cdots$			
	$\cdots$				

FIGURE 2.5
The index of coincidence of a Vigenère cipher

Now, a thorough inspection of this pattern allows us to compute the index of coincidence.

First observation: Every column is obtained by a monoalphabetic cipher, in fact by an additive cipher. Therefore, the probability that a randomly chosen pair of letters in the same column consists of equal letters is .065. Consider, on the other hand, two letters in distinct columns. Since the respective additive ciphers have been chosen "randomly," those two letters can be equal only by accident. The probability for such an event is much smaller than .065; we shall assume here that it is exactly .038. (Note that this probability is exactly $1/26 \approx .038$ if the keyword is a randomly chosen sequence of letters. If not, then the probability in question is a little bit higher; if the keyword is very long, for instance a whole paragraph, then one has to be a bit more careful.)

Second observation: Suppose one counts the number of pairs of letters that are in the same column, then the number in different columns. Let n denote the number of letters in the ciphertext. Then each column has n/l letters. (We shall generally ignore rounding errors; we assume that our text is so long that rounding errors are of no consequence.) There are precisely n possibilities for a randomly chosen letter. The chosen letter also uniquely defines its column. In that column, there are exactly $n/l - 1$ other letters; there are therefore $n/l - 1$ ways to choose the second letter. Thus, the number of pairs of letters that are *in the same column* equals

$$n \cdot \left(\frac{n}{l} - 1\right)\bigg/2 = \frac{n(n - l)}{2l}.$$

Since there are exactly $n - n/l$ letters outside the first letter's column, the number of pairs of letters that are *in different columns* equals

$$n \cdot \left(n - \frac{n}{l}\right)\bigg/2 = \frac{n^2(l - 1)}{2l}.$$

Combining the observations we see that the *expected number A of pairs of equal letters* is

$$A = \frac{n(n - l)}{2l} \cdot 0.065 + \frac{n^2(l - 1)}{2l} \cdot 0.038.$$

Therefore, the *probability* that a randomly chosen pair consists of equal letters, equals

$$\frac{A}{n(n - 1)/2} = \frac{n - l}{l(n - 1)} \cdot 0.065 + \frac{n(l - 1)}{l(n - 1)} \cdot 0.038$$

$$= \frac{1}{l(n - 1)} \cdot [0.027n + l(0.038n - 0.065)].$$

Finally, since the index of coincidence approximately equals the above probability, we get

$$I \approx \frac{0.027n}{l(n - 1)} + \frac{0.038n - 0.065}{n - 1}.$$

Stirring a little bit we obtain the desired formula, according to Friedman, for the length l of the keyword, as follows.

$$l = \frac{0.027n}{(n-1)I - 0.038n + 0.065}, \text{ where } I = \sum_{i=1}^{26} \frac{n_i(n_1 - 1)}{n(n - 1)}$$

Perhaps the formula looks complicated, and certainly its development was lengthy. But it is extremely easy to apply. Determine the length n of the text and the frequencies $n_1, \ldots, n_{26}$ of the letters. Then I and hence l can be computed automatically! It is remarkable that this ridiculously small amount of data is sufficient for a good estimate of l.

Now we apply this theory to our example. Counting the letters and their frequencies, we obtain

$$n = 491, \ \sum_{i=1}^{26} n_i^2 = 11,107.$$

Therefore we get

$$I = \frac{10,606}{240,590} = 0.044083.$$

So we can be sure that we are dealing with a polyalphabetic cipher. By the above formula we obtain also the length l of the keyword:

$$l \approx 4.34.$$

This, together with the results of the Kasiski test, indicates strongly that the length of the keyword is 5 (and not 10, 15, or 20).

Determination of the Keyword.   All this machinery enables the crypt-analyst not only to find the length of the keyword, but also the keyword itself. This is now easy.

When Mr. X knows the length l of the keyword, he knows also that the letters in positions number $1, l + 1, 2l + 1, \ldots$, or $2, l + 2, 2l + 2, \ldots$, and so forth, have been obtained using the same additive cipher. So the problem has been reduced to repeating l times the analysis of chapter 1. In order to determine the keyword (and then to decipher the ciphertext) it is often sufficient just to look for the ciphertext equivalent of the letter **e**.

In our example, $l = 5$. Among the ninety-two letters of the first mono-alphabetic part of the text, twenty-five are equal to **Z**. Thus, **e** probably corresponds to **Z**. In view of the Vigenère quadrangle we see that the first letter of the keyword is **V**. In this manner one can easily determine the keyword and then decipher the text (see exercise 5).

2.4 CONCLUDING REMARKS

We have just seen that a Vigenère cipher can be broken—and with relatively simple methods in the bargain. But can *any* Vigenère cipher be broken? No! The methods described above require a Vigenère cipher that uses a relatively short keyword.

As a consequence we must now study Vigenère ciphers having a *long* keyword. Let us not quibble over what we mean by "long." Let's go directly to the longest possible keywords: keywords as long as the cleartext. Consider two methods for designing ciphers aimed at making the cryptanalyst's life as difficult as possible.

Method 1. As keyword one can use a text from a book. Such a key has the advantage of being easy to exchange. For instance, the recipient needs only the information "Edgar Allan Poe, *The Gold Bug*," in order to decipher with the greatest of pleasure the ciphertext using the following keyword:

> Many years ago, I contracted an intimacy with a Mr. William Legrand. He was of an ancient Huguenot family, and had once been wealthy; but a series of misfortunes had reduced him to want. To avoid the mortification consequent upon his disaster, he left New Orleans, the city of his forefathers, and took up his residence at Sullivan's Island, near Charleston, South Carolina . . . .

Clearly, if one uses such a key, all methods for determining the length of the key have no effect. But since the key is an English text, statistically significant data (such as the probabilities of the letters) rub off on the ciphertext. So, an extremely clever cryptanalyst could break such a cipher. The first to observe the weakness of this cipher was, once again, Friedman, in 1920.

Method 2. The disadvantage of the previous method is that the keyword has barbs with statistics on it. Therefore we now choose as a keyword a virtually infinite sequence of randomly chosen letters (from which all statistical tests slip off like water from the back of the proverbial duck). One can think of such a sequence as being generated by an imaginary 26-sided fair die. We call this random sequence a *worm of letters*.

Such a worm has the property that knowing an arbitrarily long subsequence does not help to predict any single letter. If one enciphers a cleartext using such a worm of letters, then also the ciphertext is a purely random sequence of letters. Even if Mr. X knows an arbitrarily large amount of cleartext and of the corresponding ciphertext, he can infer from his knowledge no single further letter. In other words, such a system is even *theoretically secure*, or, in other words, it offers *perfect secrecy*. Such perfect systems will be examined closely in the next chapter.

EXERCISES

1. Construct a machine that enciphers texts using the homophonic cipher described by Table 2.1. Similarly, construct a machine for deciphering it.

@ 2. (a) Write a program that enciphers using the homophonic cipher of Table 2.1.

   (b) Using this program, encipher a relatively long text and verify whether
   i. each letter has roughly the same frequency, and
   ii. the *pairs* of letters in the ciphertext are equally distributed.

3. The homophonic cipher is only one member of a *class* of ciphers. Describe that class in such a way that it becomes clear what is the algorithm and what is the key.

4. Assume that for any letter the number of corresponding ciphertext symbols is given as in Table 2.1. Thus, we have the distribution $(12, 9, 8, 7, 7, 6, 6, 6, 6, 4, 4, 3, 3, 2, 2, 2, 2, 2, 2, 1, 1, 1, 1, 1, 1, 1)$.

   (a) How can the symbols $00, \ldots, 99$ be assigned to the letters such that
   i. any letter gets its prescribed number of ciphertext symbols, and
   ii. the assignment is random.

   @ (b) Write a program assigning the respective number of symbols to each letter in a random way.

   (c) How many assignments of the symbols $00, \ldots, 99$ to the letters are there, respecting the distribution described earlier in the exercise?

5. Determine all keyword letters of the example in section 2.3 and decipher the text.

6. The following text was obtained by a Vigenère cipher. Apply the Kasiski test to it and decipher it.

K W C S S	G X Y U T	Z B Z W U	D X Y Y J
N P R P W	O P V J J	J X V L L	T B Y U L
V O Z P W	I K Z J Z	Z Z K Y P	O T V N L
Z Z D U Q	M M G L W	N M E N E	J Z V N Z
V V F H W	K T R C F	O M O N D	Z B K Y J
C W N Y N	Z Z N Y E	P A K H G	O N F L Y
Z B K B S	O E V H W	Z L K B W	X Q G B W
M B V R L	O W U Y L	Z Z D C F	Z B Y Y U
G M R L L	Z F K O F	D Y L Y D	T E V W S
I V F N X	J Z V R S	H X C Y Z	V D V U F
V T X I J	D B Y G A	I E Y C U	C I T C H
C M I N W	S B O L W	K Z V M W	I B J Y A
O P V L H	G I Z H L	Z F K Y G	M A N C L
C W L N Z	V D Z H Y	V Z L F W	O W K Y D
G B Y Y V	Z K Z J Z	Z Z V L H	M M T C K
Z T P Q Z	Z V Z N J	Z X I Y K	Z V K M W
V V U Q Z	Z V Z N J	Z X I Y K	Z V K M K
D B Z M U	M C T C S	G B Y U L	V B V U U
C X F M A	O Q F H G	A B Y Y U	M G G N G
B Z R G C	F W N F W	Y O V I X	O P V E W
T C E C I	P M C S V	Z N Z H W	N B Y Y H
G I Z H L	Z F K Y I	P Q M U D	Z V K I X
Z I T B U	D X Y Y J	O M O N D	Z B K Y J

7. Apply the Friedman test to the text in the preceding exercise and compare the outcome to that of the Kasiski test. Explain your observation. (Hint: Compute the cleartext's index of coincidence.)

8. Is the following statement true? "It is crucial that at each position of the cleartext knowledge of the key uniquely defines the ciphertext equivalent of that cleartext letter." (See exercise 6.)

9. Can you think of a method based on statistics that can distinguish a transposition cipher from a substitution cipher?

@ 10. (a) Write a program for finding repeating sequences of letters and for determining the distances between them.

  (b) Write a program that uses the Kasiski test to determine the length of a keyword.

11. Encipher an English text (which should have at least 40 times as many letters as the keyword) using a Vigenère cipher. Transmit it to a friend (or enemy) with the invitation to break it.

12. Compute the index of coincidence of the text in exercise 20 of chapter 1.

@ 13. Write a program that
   (a) determines the length n of a given text,
   (b) computes the frequencies $n_1, \ldots, n_{26}$ of the letters in that text, and
   (c) computes the index of coincidence of the text.

14. Let $p_1, \ldots, p_{26}$ be the respective probabilities of the letters $\mathbf{a}, \ldots, \mathbf{z}$ in a text.
   (a) Prove that

$$\sum_{i=1}^{26} p_i^2 = \frac{1}{26} + \sum_{i=1}^{26} \left(p_i - \frac{1}{26} \right)^2.$$

   (b) Explain why

$$\sum_{i=1}^{26} p_i^2$$

cannot be smaller than $1/26$ ($\approx .038$) and discuss the case of equality.

@ 15. (a) Write a program that enciphers a text using a Vigenère cipher.
   (b) Design a program that breaks a text enciphered by a Vigenère cipher.

16. ¿MROWAYLLAERECNEUQESSIHTSI

17. The first polyalphabetic (or rather non-monoalphabetic) cipher was devised by Leone Battista Alberti in 1470. It made use of a device that consisted of two concentric discs comprising twenty-four cells each. (Alberti's alphabet consisted of twenty-four letters.)

Around the inner disc was the ciphertext alphabet (in random, but fixed, order). On the outer ring were the four digits 1, 2, 3, 4 and all the letters of the alphabet except the four with least probability, k, j, q, and x. Sender and recipient had to agree upon a letter, the so-called *indicator*.

For enciphering, the sender fixed arbitrarily the position of the outer ring. He looked for the indicator (as a letter of the outer ring) and wrote as the first letter of the ciphertext the ciphertext letter corresponding to the indicator. The sender proceeded by enciphering the cleartext as if it were a monoalphabetic cipher. (If, by accident, one of the letters k, j, q, x occurred in the cleartext, it was simply omitted.)

Whenever the sender wanted to change the correspondence, he chose one of the numbers 1, 2, 3, or 4 and recorded as the next letter of his ciphertext the corresponding ciphertext letter. He then rotated the ring so that the ciphertext letter that had corresponded to the chosen number now corresponded to the indicator.

(a) Build yourself a model and encipher a message.

(b) Devise a deciphering method.

(c) What are the advantages of this "Alberti algorithm" over, for instance, a Vigenère cipher?

(d) What are the keys in the Alberti algorithm?

(e) How secure is this algorithm?

Additional information. A modification of the Alberti algorithm was used by the Italian army until after World War II. (Don't get excited! This code was only used to "superencrypt" already enciphered messages.)

18. Take the rest of the day off and read Edgar Allan Poe's "The Gold Bug." (In this short story the cryptanalysis of a monoalphabetic cipher based on statistical analysis plays a central role!)

Chapter 3

SAFETY FIRST
or
A LITTLE BIT OF THEORY

> Many a man applies his intellect to simplify,
> many to complicate.
>
> —Erich Kästner

The aim of this chapter is to firm up the foundations for the ideas I have been discussing. Here we shall consider the meaning of a "perfectly secure" cipher system, inevitably leading us to practical systems. Although in discussing perfect systems I cannot avoid probabilistic arguments, I can make do with only the most elementary notions; usually it suffices to know that "the probability" is a number between 0 and 1.

3.1 CIPHER SYSTEMS

We now consider cipher systems—families of cleartexts with their possible ciphertexts, algorithms and keys. Of course, for true precision and clarity such objects would have to be treated axiomatically; it is better for our purposes, however, to explain these objects by means of typical examples.

A typical family of cleartexts might be the New York Public Library's collection of British novels between 1800 and 1900. A cipher system could be made up of these texts, together with all 312 affine ciphers (described in section 1.4) and the resulting ciphertexts. For another example take as cleartexts all Latin sentences composed of not more than ten Latin words, all twenty-six additive ciphers and all resulting ciphertexts.

We shall need lots of notation. By M (for messages) we will denote the set of cleartexts (in our above examples the collection of novels or the Latin sentences). The set of all keys—we don't need a name for it—is in our first example the set of all pairs (s, t), s being one of the twenty-six shifts and t one of the twelve possible multipliers. Finally C is the collection of all ciphertexts (in the first example 312 of them for each novel).

An easier, but less typical cipher system is shown in Figure 3.1.

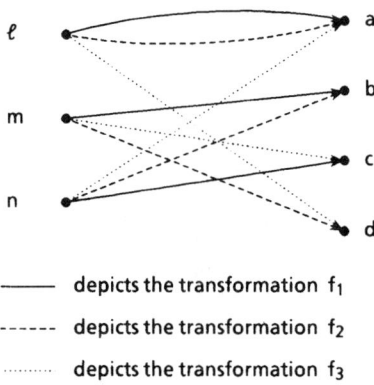

—— depicts the transformation f_1

- - - - - depicts the transformation f_2

········· depicts the transformation f_3

FIGURE 3.1
A cipher system

M contains the three cleartexts l, m, n. We'll denote the size of a set by a pair of vertical lines, so $|M| = 3$. C is composed of the four texts a, b, c, d—therefore, $|C| = 4$. The algorithm is depicted in the figure by the arrows and labeled by the letter f with a subscript—1, 2, or 3—that represents the key. Thus, for example, $f_1(l) = a, f_1(m) = b, f_1(n) = c$.

In general, we denote by f the cipher algorithm. If sender and receiver have agreed upon a key k, then they obtain a specialization f_k of the algorithm f. Hence we obtain for any key k a specialization f_k of f. These mappings f_k from M into C are called *transformations*. The set of all these transformations is F. So $|F| = 3$ in the example of Figure 3.1.

What are the properties of the mappings $f_k \in F$? A quite natural requirement is that the receiver must be able to decipher the ciphertext $f_k(m)$.

Therefore there must be a mapping f_k^{-1} with the property that

$$f_k^{-1}(f_k(m)) = m \text{ for all } m \in M.$$

In other words, any ciphertext $f_k(m)$ can by deciphered by applying f_k^{-1}. A transformation with this property is said to be *invertible*.

Now we can define a cipher system. This definition goes back to the American mathematician Claude E. Shannon (born 1916), not only the father of information theory, but also of modern cryptology [Sha49].

A *symmetric cipher system S* consists of a set M of cleartexts, a set C of ciphertexts, and a set F of invertible transformations from M into C. We write $S = (M, C, F)$. (See Figure 3.2.)

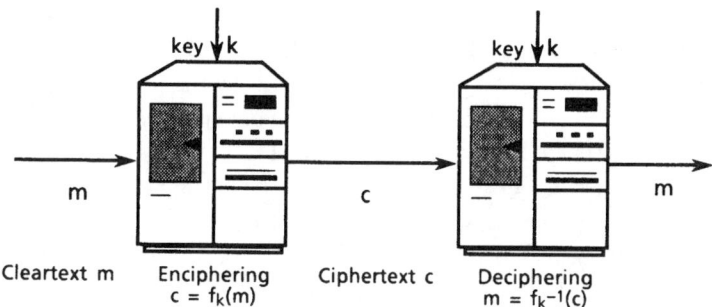

Cleartext m   Enciphering   Ciphertext c   Deciphering
$c = f_k(m)$ $m = f_k^{-1}(c)$

FIGURE 3.2
A symmetric cipher system

Before we run out of letters, we shall pause for a closer look at the example described by Figure 3.1. This example shows us two things.

- Two different transformations (in our example f_1 and f_2) are allowed to map the same cleartext onto the same ciphertext.
- The fact that a transformation f_k is invertible means that at no point on the right hand side (that is, at no ciphertext) can there arrive two arrows named f_k. (Otherwise this ciphertext could not be deciphered uniquely.) It follows that there must be at least as many c's as m's: $|M| \leq |C|$.

The reader is invited to construct his own cipher systems, even some exotic ones.

3.2 PERFECT SECURITY

Now we know what a cipher system is, but not yet what makes it secure or insecure. The main aim of this section is to describe precisely what a secure cipher system is. Since we are interested not only in secure but also in perfect ciphers, we must also define those systems.

Intuitively speaking, perfect security means that the cryptanalyst Mr. X has no chance to increase his knowledge of the system; even if he employs all the world's know-how and computing power Mr. X knows no more than when he started. Throughout the previous chapters we have observed that cryptanalysis relies very much on probabilities. It should come as no surprise that probability will play a crucial role in the present discussion. For a cleartext μ denote by $p(\mu)$ its probability.

Examples. (a) Suppose the cleartexts of M are the *letters* of the words in a typical English book; in the format of Figure 3.1 the letters o, n, c, e, u, p, o, n, a, t, i, m, e, ... would be listed in a column down the left side of the diagram. Then if the message μ of interest is the letter **e**, the probability $p(\mu)$ would be simply the relative frequency of the letter **e**; thus, according to Table 1.2, $p(\mu) = p(\mathbf{e})$ would be about 0.127.

(b) Suppose that M consists of all consecutive pairs of letters from the words of a typical English book; in our standard format all the pairs (on, nc, ce, eu, up, po, on, na, at, ti, im, me, ...) would be listed in a column. When μ is a particular bigram (pair of consecutive letters), $p(\mu)$ is the frequency of the bigram in that book. As mentioned in section 1.6, *he* is the most frequent bigram in common English, with a frequency exceeding 0.03.

These numbers $p(\mu)$ are called *a priori* (or *theoretical*) probabilities; they are, of course, known to the cryptanalyst.

Let us now assume that Mr. X has intercepted a ciphertext γ. In order to analyze γ he could—at least in principle—review all cleartexts μ and in each case compute the probability that γ was obtained from μ. We shall denote these so-called *a posteriori* (or *observed*) probabilities by $p_\gamma(\mu)$.

Examples. (c) Let M be as in example (a) above, the letters of the words of a typical English book, and let the algorithm be the additive ciphers (with each of the twenty-six possible keys). Fitting the information of Table 1.1 (which displays the additive ciphers) into the format of Figure 3.1, we list the letters of the book in order down the left side of the diagram. From each letter twenty-six arrows emanate (one for each key) to the twenty-six enciphered letters—those listed in the column beneath the cleartext letter in Table 1.1. (Thus there are twenty-six times as many letters down the right side of the diagram as down the left. See Figure 3.3.)

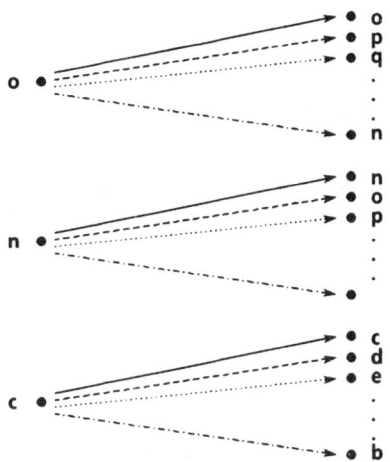

FIGURE 3.3
The cipher system for example (c)

Observe that each ciphertext letter, denoted by γ, has an equal chance of coming from any particular cleartext letter—so in about 12.7% of the occurrences of γ on the right it is the cipher equivalent of the letter e; in 8.167% of the occurrences it corresponds to **a**, and so forth. In other words,

given any ciphertext γ, $p_\gamma(\mu) = p(\mu)$ for any cleartext μ!

(d) Let each cleartext of M consist of the first 100 letters on a page of Volume 1 of the *Encyclopedia Britanica*—so that $|M|$ is the number of pages in that volume—and again let the algorithm consist of the additive ciphers. The picture now has the blocks of 100 letters stacked up in a huge column on the left; from each block there are twenty-six arrows, each to the corresponding block of ciphertext. For any $\mu \in M$ the probability is $p(\mu) = 1/|M|$, which is a small but positive number. Since it is easy to check whether or not a particular ciphertext γ came from a particular μ (the distribution of letters in γ must exactly match the distribution of the corresponding letters in μ), it follows that $p_\gamma(\mu)$ equals either 1 or 0. Thus,

given any ciphertext γ, $p_\gamma(\mu) \neq p(\mu)$ *for any cleartext* μ!

Let's look more carefully at the last example. If the cryptanalyst Mr. X were to find for a certain μ

$$p_\gamma(\mu) > p(\mu),$$

then he would conclude that the probability of finding μ by analyzing γ is better than the probability of choosing it at random among the cleartexts in M. Thus there would be some chance that γ came from μ.

Similarly, if

$$p_\gamma(\mu) < p(\mu),$$

then Mr. X would know that there is only a small probability that γ had been obtained by enciphering μ. So, also in this case, he would have increased his knowledge.

Therefore we define: A cipher system S offers *perfect security* if for *each* ciphertext γ we have

$$p_\gamma(\mu) = p(\mu)$$

for all cleartexts μ. In other words: S is perfectly secure if the a priori and the a posteriori probabilities are always equal. This is what happens in example (c); *the additive ciphers are perfect when acting on single letters*! Mr. X may work as hard as he can without obtaining any information; the letter of the ciphertext is essentially chosen at random.

So far, so perfect. But are there perfect systems? More to the point, how can a perfect system be recognized as such? What we clearly desire are easy-to-check criteria that tell us whether or not a given cipher system S offers perfect security.

Criterion 1. *If* **S** *has perfect security, then any cleartext of the system can be translated using a key of* **S** *into any ciphertext of the system.*

In other words, the diagram representing a perfect system in the spirit of Figure 3.1 would have each point on the left-hand side connected by at least one arrow to each ciphertext of **S**.

Why is this criterion true? Consider a cleartext μ and a ciphertext γ.
First observation: Since **S** is perfect, by definition $p_\gamma(\mu) = p(\mu)$.

Second observation: In any system we have $p(\mu) > 0$, since any cleartext has a certain (perhaps very small, but still positive) probability. Together it follows $p_\gamma(\mu) > 0$.

What does this mean? This means that there is at least one key that transfers μ into γ (if there were no such key, then necessarily $p_\gamma(\mu) = 0$). This already ends the proof of the first criterion.

This criterion is very useful—in a negative sense; it enables us to check that certain systems are *not* perfect. For instance, the cipher system of Figure 3.1 is certainly not perfect—among other things, l is not connected to b. Also, the claim that the system described in example (d) is not perfect could be based on criterion 1.

Criterion 2. *If* **S** *is perfect, then*

$$|F| \geq |C| \geq |M|.$$

We have already observed that $|C| \geq |M|$ is true in any cipher system, whether it is perfect or not.

Why must $|F| \geq |C|$? In order to convince ourselves of this fact, we fix a cleartext μ and encipher μ using all possible transformations of **S**. In view of the first criterion, μ can be mapped onto any ciphertext. At the same time, for each ciphertext a different transformation is needed (since a single transformation cannot map μ onto γ and at the same time onto $\gamma' \neq \gamma$). Therefore the number of transformations needed is at least as big as the number of ciphertexts. In other words, $|F| \geq |C|$.

Now we turn the tables. The following criterion makes it possible to produce perfect cipher systems enough and to spare. The proof of this fact is not exactly difficult, but one needs some experience in fiddling around with probabilities. The reader who is interested in proving the criterion will find comfort and help in the exercises.

Criterion 3. *Let* **S** $= (M, C, F)$ *be a cipher system with*

$$|F| = |C| = |M|,$$

in which all keys occur with the same probability. Furthermore, we suppose *that for any cleartext μ and any ciphertext γ there is exactly one transformation of* **S** *mapping μ onto γ. Then* **S** *is perfect!*

As stated before, using this criterion one can construct perfect systems in the most simple way. Figure 3.4 shows an example. (The four different transformations are indicated by the different styles of arrows.)

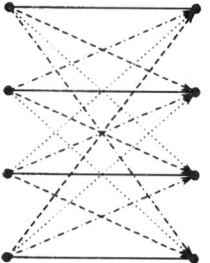

FIGURE 3.4
A perfect cipher

3.3 THE ONE-TIME PAD

Now I shall present a perfect system of great importance to both the theory and practice of ciphers.

The cleartexts consist of combinations of letters of an arbitrary but fixed length n. As keys we choose all 26^n sequences of letters of length n; we assume that these keys occur with the same probability. Enciphering a cleartext $a_1 a_2 \ldots a_n$ proceeds according to the scheme described in Figure 3.5.

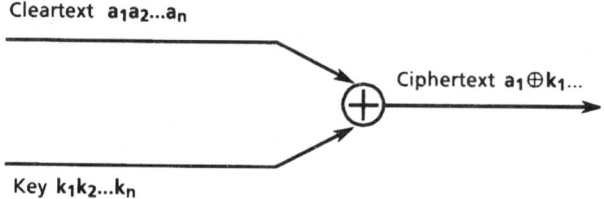

Cleartext $a_1 a_2 \ldots a_n$

Ciphertext $a_1 \oplus k_1 \ldots$

Key $k_1 k_2 \ldots k_n$

FIGURE 3.5
The Vernam cipher

The ith cleartext letter $\mathbf{a}_i$ will be added to the keyletter $\mathbf{k}_i$; in other words, $\mathbf{a}_i$ will be enciphered using the additive cipher alphabet that starts with the letter $\mathbf{k}_i$. In the language of Chapter 2, one enciphers the text $\mathbf{a}_1\mathbf{a}_2 \ldots \mathbf{a}_n$ using a Vigenère cipher with the key word $\mathbf{k}_1\mathbf{k}_2 \ldots \mathbf{k}_n$.

Using Criterion 3 above, we can convince ourselves that *this cipher system provides perfect secrecy*. The set of cleartexts, the set of ciphertexts, and the set of all keys coincide (for all these sets consist of all sequences of n letters); in particular,

$$|F| = |C| = |M|.$$

Thus the first condition of Criterion 3 has already been verified. In order to check the second condition we recall that for any cleartext $\mu = \mathbf{a}_1\mathbf{a}_2 \ldots \mathbf{a}_n$ and any ciphertext $\gamma = \mathbf{c}_1\mathbf{c}_2 \ldots \mathbf{c}_n$ there is exactly one key $k = \mathbf{k}_1\mathbf{k}_2 \ldots \mathbf{k}_n$ transforming μ into γ. (Since this will be performed letter-by-letter, it is sufficient to check this property for a cleartext letter $\mathbf{a}_i$ and a ciphertext letter $\mathbf{c}_i$—but then the condition follows directly from the definition of a Vigenère cipher.)

Hence, both hypotheses of the third criterion are fulfilled. As a consequence, our system is perfect: it is unbreakable!

This system was proposed in 1917 by the American AT&T engineer Gilbert S. Vernam (1890–1960); it is commonly called the *one-time pad*. Formerly the key letters were written across each page of a pad of paper; once a key letter had been used, the corresponding page was simply torn off.

Today, the one-time pad is not used with letters on a pad, but with bits on a computer (see Figure 3.6). Then the $\mathbf{a}_i$ and $\mathbf{k}_i$ are bits and the ciphertext $\mathbf{a}_1 \oplus \mathbf{k}_1, \mathbf{a}_2 \oplus \mathbf{k}_2, \ldots$ is obtained by adding bit-by-bit modulo 2—that is, using the rule

$$1 \oplus 1 = 0 \oplus 0 = 0; \; 1 \oplus 0 = 0 \oplus 1 = 1.$$

We shall meet this operation again in the next section.

For the security of this system it is crucial that all sequences of length n occur as the key with the same probability. In other words, *the key bits must be chosen at random*. The best way to imagine this is by flipping a fair coin n times (head = 1, tails = 0). Of course, there are faster methods. In practice one might use a physical random source and produce the random bits automatically.

Cleartext

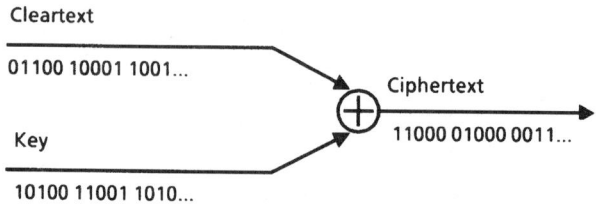

01100 10001 1001...

Ciphertext

Key

11000 01000 0011...

10100 11001 1010...

FIGURE 3.6
The One-Time Pad

The price paid for this form of perfect secrecy is high in terms of both dollars and resources. The one-time pad generates an enormous amount of paper, all of which must be kept from intruders twenty-four hours each day. For this reason the system is used sparingly. During World War II, for example, it was used by the codebreakers of Bletchley Park to send to the Prime Minister the messages they decoded from the German ENIGMA—in that way the Allies were able to keep the Germans from knowing that their ENIGMA code had been broken. (See [Kah67].)

It is rumored that the "hot line" between the White House and the Kremlin during the heat of the cold war was secured by an electronic one-time pad. However, the same unconfirmed rumors say that the system was used only for test purposes by service personnel. These days, more than one algorithm is used, one of which is based on a one-time pad.

To look more closely at why this undoubtedly perfect system is used so seldom let's take the recipient's point of view. Of course, he can decipher the ciphertext with ease; deciphering is essentially the same as enciphering. (If one uses the binary one-time pad, it is exactly the same as enciphering.) Well, he can decipher leisurely—but only when he has the key!

Is there a problem?

The transmission of a long secret key is indeed a serious problem since, by definition, the key has to be transmitted secretly. If one transmits it the same way as the ciphertext, then the chance that the key is read is as great as the chance that the ciphertext is intercepted, since the key has the same length as the ciphertext. Does this mean that one could save time and trouble by simply sending the clear message directly to the recipient? *No*, since the sender can choose a more convenient *means* or a more convenient *time* for transmitting the key.

A different means would be, for instance, to send the key via courier. Of course, the latter bears a certain risk; he lives in danger and perhaps not very long. More importantly, the sender can choose the time of the key exchange; he seldom has any choice for the time when the actual message must be sent. The example of the hot line makes this quite clear. The tapes that contain the key were transported in tranquility by the members of the diplomatic corps. When a crisis arose, the U.S. President and Soviet Premier were able to exchange pleasantries by phone without the danger that someone could listen to their conversation. In any case, it was not some complex key exchange procedure that caused any breakdown in communications.

3.4 SHIFT REGISTERS

One can discuss ad nauseam the problem of exchanging keys; in fact it is not just a theoretical problem, but also a very serious bottleneck. In chapter 5 we shall present new and very good protocols for key exchange. But it remains extremely difficult to overcome these difficulties in the case of the one-time pad.

One important attempt to solve this problem is to replace the truly random sequence by a sequence that is only *pseudorandom*. Such a sequence looks at first glance (and sometimes also at second glance) as if it were truly random, but it isn't; what's more, it is determined by very few parameters. Thus, the sender has to transmit only these few parameters, which provide the key in a strict sense. Both communication partners can then compute from the parameters the pseudorandom sequence and, using this sequence, they are able to encipher and to decipher. Clearly such a procedure does not solve the key exchange problem, but it disarms it in an essential way (see Figure 3.7).

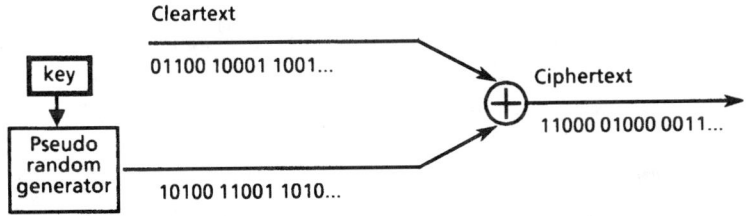

FIGURE 3.7
Pseudorandom generator

Of course, one has to pay for this advantage: Such systems are no longer perfectly secure. So one has to compromise between security and the amount of data transmitted. For the remainder of this chapter we shall examine a most important method of generating pseudorandom sequences, and some of the problems involved.

A pseudorandom key is a pseudorandom sequence of numbers. As is the case with random sequences, $(0, 1)$ sequences are nearly always used. For cryptographic purposes most of these pseudorandom sequences are generated by *shift registers*. There are two reasons for this.

- Shift registers can be realized very efficiently by computer hardware.
- The mathematical theory of shift registers has seen considerable development over the last 20 years and is relatively well understood. As a consequence, methods have been developed for quantifying the cryptographic effectiveness of a given shift register.

At first glance, a shift register looks rather technical (as a technical device should), but let's not let that bother us.

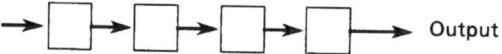 Output

This diagram represents a *shift register* of *length* 4; it consists of four cells in series, each of which is able to store one bit—that is, a 0 or a 1. The shift register is controlled by a clock; at a specified time, the content of each cell is shifted (in the direction of the arrow) to the next cell. More precisely, the rightmost cell (the "first" cell) outputs its bit and receives the content of the second cell. The latter receives the bit from the third cell; finally the last (i.e., leftmost) cell transmits its bit to the third cell.

Were the shift register to perform only these operations, the procedure would be *unjust* (since the last cell would give away its bit without compensation) and *boring* (since, after four ticks of the clock, the register would be empty).

In short, the last cell must be kept alive with a bit from somewhere. From where? And which bit? At first one may be tempted to argue as follows: The first cell should not only output its bit, but should at the same time feed it into the last cell.

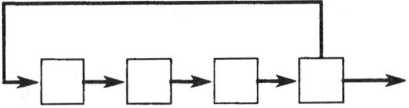

This is indeed a good idea: one has to feed back! But the idea is, in general, too naive. For the shift register would then reproduce periodically the initial states of the cells. This is useless for cryptographic purposes, where patterns of any kind are always to be avoided.

So maybe the last cell should get input not only from the first cell, but also from others? The question is: From which cells, and what? This is, indeed, the question.

For a *linear feedback* shift register the question has been answered as follows. A particular set of cells is chosen; their states will be added and fed into the last cell. Again we use the rules

$$0 \oplus 0 = 0, \ 1 \oplus 0 = 1, \ 0 \oplus 1 = 1, \ 1 \oplus 1 = 0.$$

The mathematician would call this simplest of all additions an *addition modulo 2*, whereas the technician simply says that this $\oplus$ is the *XOR* operation (*exclusive or*, from its use in logic). The following figure shows a typical linear feedback shift register of length 4:

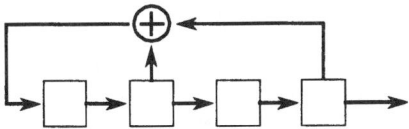

In this shift register the feedback is organized in such a way that the sum of the contents of the first and third cell is fed into the last cell. Those cells at the start of an upward arrow are the distinguished cells that contribute to the last cell's content; the others are pure worker cells (what little they have at time i is taken away at time $i + 1$).

The value fed back into the last cell is called the *feedback*; the shift register is called *linear* because the feedback rule is as simple as possible: mere addition. Of course one can use for the feedback more than two cells; the following shift register has the property that its feedback is the sum of the first three cells.

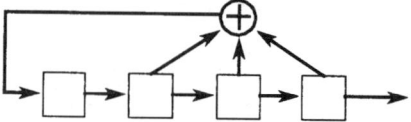

Now the time has come to study examples; we shall simultaneously consider two shift registers of length 4.

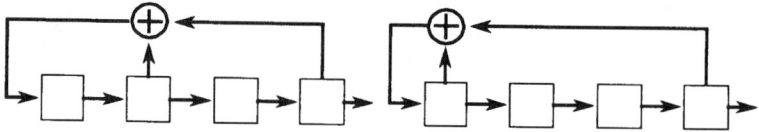

Let's start! How? O.K., any shift register needs an *initialization*. In other words, no cell can be empty. Each cell needs a 0 or a 1. Let's choose for both shift registers the same initialization, say 1000, and observe the change of the states until the pattern emerges.

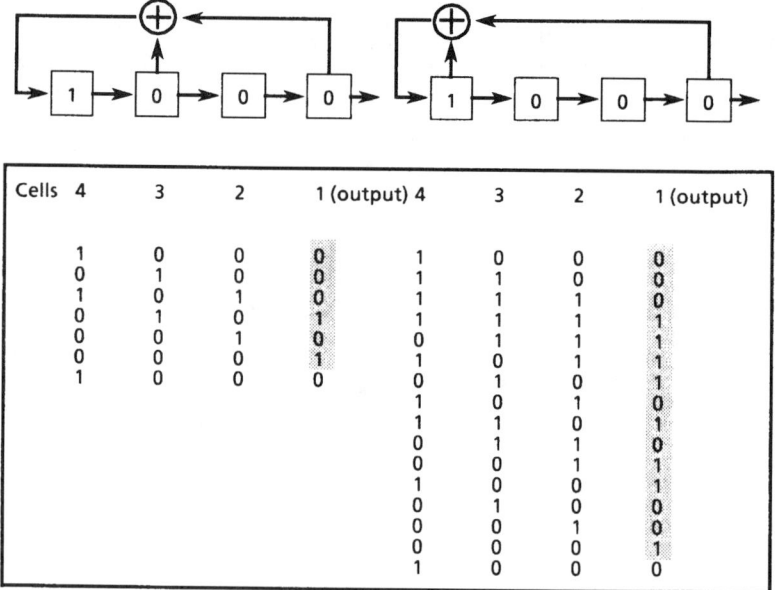

Cells	4	3	2	1 (output)	4	3	2	1 (output)
	1	0	0	0	1	0	0	0
	0	1	0	0	1	1	0	0
	1	0	1	0	1	1	1	0
	0	1	0	1	1	1	1	1
	0	0	1	0	0	1	1	1
	0	0	0	1	1	0	1	1
	1	0	0	0	0	1	0	1
					1	0	1	0
					1	1	0	1
					0	1	1	0
					0	0	1	1
					1	0	0	1
					0	1	0	0
					0	0	1	0
					0	0	0	1
					1	0	0	0

The respective pseudorandom sequences consist of those bits that come from the first cell. Therefore, the first shift register produces the sequence

$$0001010001010...,$$

whereas the second gives the output sequence

$$0001111010110010001111010110010...$$

Note that the sequences repeat after a certain time. They are *periodic*, the period being the number of steps until the first repetition starts. For instance, the first sequence has period 6; the second, period 15. It is clear that a long period is desirable—the pattern is harder to detect. We shall soon see, however, that the security suggested by a relatively long period is deceptive.

How long can the period of a linear shift register be? Alternatively, how many distinct states can a shift register have? Since (in our example) any state is a quadruple of zeroes and ones, one can also ask: How many distinct quadruples of 0's and 1's are there? But this is an easy question. The number of binary 4-tuples is $2^4 = 16$.

However, in linear shift registers one state plays a peculiar role, or more precisely, no role at all. This is the state in which all cells have value 0. When the shift register consists of all zeroes, then it remains forever in that state. Therefore, in order to achieve a maximum period, the zero state must not occur. Consequently, we revise our estimate for the maximum period of a linear shift register of length 4 to be $2^4 - 1 = 15$. The above example shows that there exist shift registers that realize this theoretical maximum.

Mathematicians are able to provide criteria for a shift register of length n to have the maximum period. In particular it has been proved that for every positive integer n there is a linear shift register of maximal period $2^n - 1$. The reader is referred to the literature [BP82, Rue86] for more information. You will certainly find it more instructive, however, to construct—without any theory—your own linear shift registers of maximum period (see exercise 14).

3.5 CRYPTANALYSIS OF LINEAR FEEDBACK SHIFT REGISTERS

Wonderful! We may employ linear shift registers in order to generate pseudo-random sequences for cryptographic purposes. This is economical! Linear shift registers are high-performance tools. What more do we want?

True, sequences from a linear shift register have undeniably excellent statistical properties; this holds even for sequences generated by relatively short linear shift registers, and that is the good news. The bad news is that, from a cryptological point of view, these sequences have a rather doubtful character; they are by no means resistant to a known plaintext attack.

Suppose that the cryptanalyst Mr. X knows that a cipher was the product of a linear shift register of length 4. His task is to reconstruct the key, which consists of the initialization and the exact feedback rule. Imagine, moreover, that Mr. X knows of a sequence of eight cleartext bits and the corresponding ciphertext bits. Adding those bits he gets an eight-bit subsequence of the key stream produced by the (unknown!) shift register. Take as an example the sequence

$$0\ 0\ 0\ 1\ 1\ 1\ 1\ 0.$$

Remember how a shift register works: The first output bits are just the initial state of the cells. Since the shift register under investigation has length 4, the four leftmost bits of the sequence are the initial states. That is, before the sequence was released, the register looked like the following.

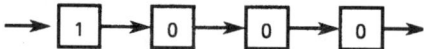

This is the easier half of Mr. X's task. The second half is to determine the feedback coefficients. To this end, he provisionally provides an arrow up from every cell, assigning the ith arrow the label c_i. Each c_i takes the value 1 or 0. If $c_i = 1$, then the corresponding arrow is really there and the cell i influences the feedback; if $c_i = 0$, then there is no such arrow. Schematically, the shift register looks as follows.

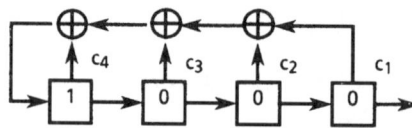

For instance, in the two examples just considered we had, respectively, $c_1 = 1, c_2 = 0, c_3 = 1, c_4 = 0$, and $c_1 = 1, c_2 = 0, c_3 = 0, c_4 = 1$. Now Mr. X has a clearly defined task: he must determine the values of the c_i's. In order to do this, he must study the behavior of the shift register over several units of time. After the first time interval, the shift register has the following appearance:

State of cell 4	State of cell 3	State of cell 2	State of cell 1
c_4	1	0	0

After the next, in the leftmost cell we have the entry $c_4 \cdot c_4 \oplus c_3$. Here we use binary multiplication, namely,

$$1 \cdot 1 = 1, \; 1 \cdot 0 = 0 \cdot 1 = 0 \cdot 0 = 0.$$

In particular we have $c_4 \cdot c_4 = c_4$. Hence the state of the shift register at the second stage (after one unit of time) is

State of cell 4	State of cell 3	State of cell 2	State of cell 1
$c_4 \oplus c_3$	c_4	1	0

And so forth. At time 3 one finds in cell 4 a complicated expression that, luckily, simplifies:

$$c_2 \oplus c_3 \cdot c_4 \oplus c_4 \cdot (c_4 \oplus c_3) = c_2 \oplus c_3 \cdot c_4 \oplus c_4 \cdot c_4 \oplus c_4 \cdot c_3 = c_2 \oplus c_4.$$

(The familiar rules of arithmetic still hold in the binary system, but beyond that you must remember that $x \oplus x = 0$ and $x \cdot x = x$ for $x = 0$ or 1.)

State of cell 4	State of cell 3	State of cell 2	State of cell 1
$c_2 \oplus c_4$	$c_3 \oplus c_4$	c_4	1

And at time 4 matters seem complicated beyond hope:

State of cell 4	State of cell 3	State of cell 2	State of cell 1
$c_1 \oplus c_3 \oplus c_4 \oplus c_3 \cdot c_4$	$c_2 \oplus c_4$	$c_3 \oplus c_4$	c_4

But now there is no need for any further exploration; in the next four moves, the output bits will just be those states shown in the boxes above (in turn from right to left).

But Mr. X already knows these output bits—they are the remaining bits of the sequence of length 8. Therefore Mr. X knows that

$$c_4 = 1,$$

$$c_3 \oplus c_4 = 1,$$

$$c_2 \oplus c_4 = 1, \text{and}$$

$$c_1 \oplus c_3 \oplus c_4 \oplus c_3 \cdot c_4 = 0.$$

Thus, he obtains without any difficulty

$$c_4 = 1, \ c_3 = 0, \ c_2 = 0, \text{ and } c_1 = 1,$$

and he recovers our shift register with period 15:

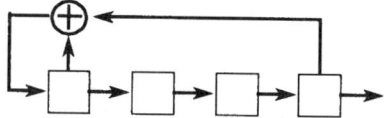

One can prove in general that Mr. X can break a linear shift register of length n (hence of maximal period $2^n - 1$) if he knows a sequence of $2n$ successive bits of corresponding cleartext and ciphertext. This is a spectacular result; for instance, a sequence that repeats only after one million (precisely $1,048,575 = 2^{20} - 1$) bits can be reconstructed from just forty of its bits!

What now? Is the whole idea of shift registers nonsense? Perhaps it was *too* nice; shift registers can be realized with extreme ease and produce pseudorandom sequences with breathtaking speed. (10,000,000 bits per second presents no problem at all.) One would like to keep these beautiful features, while at the same time coping with the cryptographic weaknesses.

This is done by employing nonlinear feedback shift registers. These shift registers use a more intricate, nonlinear feedback rule R, with multiplication and addition of the bits all mixed together.

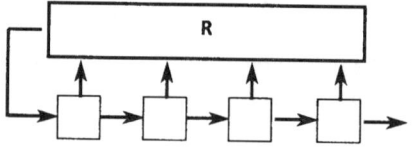

As a simple example we consider the following shift register of length 4.

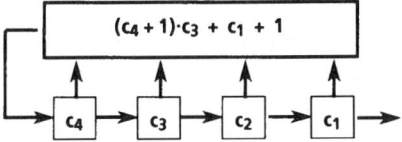

One easily sees that this shift register is not a linear shift register, since the zero state is transformed into a nonzero state (see also exercises 19 and 20). Of course, even nonlinear feedback shift registers fail to provide perfect security in the strict sense of section 3.2, but they are better than the linear sequences. In fact, most crypto algorithms these days make use of nonlinear shift registers—though the most popular single algorithm is certainly the DES.

There is one fundamental question that I should discuss before closing this chapter: *How can one measure the cryptologic quality of a* $(0, 1)$ *sequence?* We have seen that the period is an unreliable tool. In a way, the *linear complexity* is such a measure. Clearly, any periodic $(0, 1)$ sequence (of period p, say) can be obtained from a linear shift register; the stupidest thing to do is to take a shift register of length p, write the sequence in question as the initial state in the register, and feed only the rightmost cell back to the last cell. Often, there will be a shorter linear shift register producing this sequence. For instance, any sequence of maximal period $p = 2^n - 1$ obtained from a linear shift register of length n serves as an example with $n \approx \log p$.

The *linear complexity* of a sequence is the minimum length of a linear shift register producing the sequence as part of its output sequence. The greater its linear complexity, the better the sequence is for cryptographic purposes. But beware: A large linear complexity is only a necessary condition for the cryptographic strength of a sequence.

There are useful methods of computing the linear complexity of a sequence, among which is the *Berlekamp-Massey algorithm* ([Mas68], see also [Rue86]—this is recommended reading for those with a working knowledge of linear algebra and binary arithmetic).

EXERCISES

1. Construct a few cipher systems by defining the set of cleartexts, the set of transformations, and the set of ciphertexts.

2. Count the frequencies of letters in a text of a foreign language. What are the main differences from the corresponding frequencies in English?

3. How many sequences of length 3 of the twenty-six letters are there if
   (a) one allows all combinations;
   (b) one considers only proper English words? (Hint: More than 50.)

4. An operating system accepts for user authentication passwords consisting of exactly four alphanumeric symbols.
   (a) What is the total number of possible passwords?
   (b) How many passwords are possible if every password must contain at least one digit and at least one letter?
   (c) Compare the numbers obtained in (a) and (b) with the number of the first names you know.
   (d) Which system, (a) or (b), would you choose if you would like to have a large number of actually used passwords?

5. The example of Figure 3.1 can be enlarged by further transformations. Find at least four further transformations.

6. (a) How many invertible transformations from M into C are there, if $|M| = 3$ and $|C| = 5$?
   (b) Solve the same problem when $|M| = 1066$ and $|C| = 1776$.

7. Prove that a cipher system S is perfect if and only if for all cleartexts m one has $p_m(c) = p(c)$ for all ciphertexts c.

8. Construct a cipher system $S = (M, C, K)$, with $|K| > |C| > |M|$, that is not perfect.

▷▷ 9. In a statistics textbook, look up the formula of Bayes and prove the third criterion of section 3.2. (Hint: Use exercise 7.)

10. Convince yourself that the following methods yield random sequences.
    (a) Rolling a fair die. If an odd number is encoded by 1 and an even number is encoded by 0, one gets a binary random sequence.
    (b) Spinning a roulette wheel. This yields a random sequence in which every element can have thirty-seven values (numbers $0, 1, \ldots, 36$).

11. Have you ever seen a 20-sided fair die? (Hint: Look at the front cover of this book.)

12. Construct a linear shift register of length 4 that transmits a nonzero state into the zero state.

13. Convince yourself of the following fact. If a linear shift register has maximum period, then there is an arrow starting from the rightmost cell (that is, this cell contributes actively to the feedback).

14. Construct linear shift registers with maximum period of lengths 3, 5, and 6.

15. The following output sequence was obtained from a linear feedback shift register of length 5.

$$0\ 0\ 0\ 0\ 1\ 0\ 0\ 0\ 1\ 1$$

Reconstruct the shift register.

16. You are told that the following output sequence comes from a linear shift register of length 4.

$$0\ 0\ 0\ 0\ 1\ 0\ 0\ 0$$

Would you like to comment on this statement?

17. Write down some binary sequence of length 10 and try to compute a shift register of length 5 having this sequence as part of its output sequence.

18. (a) Construct a nonlinear feedback function for a shift register of length 4.
    (b) Determine whether the sequence produced by the shift register of (a) can be produced by a linear feedback shift register of length 4.

19. Show that the shift register claimed to be nonlinear (the last diagram of section 3.5) is indeed not equivalent to any linear shift register of length 4. (For example, you can show that Mr. X's method leads to a self-contradictory set of equations.)

20. Which of the following feedback rules describe a nonlinear feedback shift register?

$$c_4 c_1 + c_3 + 1$$

$$(c_4 + 1)c_3 + (c_3 + 1)c_2 + c_1 + 1$$

$$(c_4 + 1)c_3 + (c_3 + 1)c_2 + c_1$$

$$(c_4 + 1)c_3 + (c_4 + 1)(c_3 + 1)c_2 + c_1 + 1$$

21. Is there a shift register of length 4 producing an output sequence of period 16? (Look at the examples of the preceding exercise.)

Additional information. When talking about an algorithm's key size, which contains, for instance, 56, 64, 128, or even more bits, some people argue, "O.K., but—if I am lucky, I can guess the key!"

Let's analyze this statement. Of course, one has to admit that in a theoretical sense it is true. More precisely, the probability of guessing a 64-bit key is $1/2^{64}$, a number that, granted, is greater than zero. But, let us compare this number with numbers we are used to. First, observe that

$$2^{64} \approx 1.84 \cdot 10^{19}.$$

In other words, guessing the key is equivalent to choosing one prescribed element out of a set of more than 10^{19} elements. Can you imagine this last number? Let me help with a few illustrations.

- The world population is now about 6 billion, or $6 \cdot 10^9$. Since there are roughly as many women as men, one can form $(3 \cdot 10^9) \cdot (3 \cdot 10^9) = 9 \cdot 10^{18}$ couples. So, the number of all possible man and woman couples is smaller than the number of all 64-bit keys.
- In one drop (cubic millimeter) of water there are about 10^{19} molecules. So guessing the key is as difficult as fishing at random a particular molecule out of a drop of water. (This number becomes even more impressive if the key consists of about 80 bits. Then guessing the key is equivalent to fishing a particular molecule out of a pint of water.)
- The number of choices in Lotto 6-49 is 13,983,816 $\approx 10^7$ (the number of ways to choose six numbers between 1 and 49). So the chance of guessing the right 64-bit key is something like winning the grand prize in Lotto 6-49 this week, next week and the following week. Moral: If by guessing the key you expect to gain only a couple of million dollars, you'd be better off buying a lottery ticket.

Chapter 4

MAC DATA
or
A WATCHDOG CALLED AUTHENTICATION

...The King had Allerleirauh brought before
him. He espied the white finger and saw the ring
which he had put on it during the dance. Then
he grasped her by the hand and held her fast,
and when she moved to release herself and run
away, her fur mantle opened a bit, and the star
dress shone forth. The King clutched the mantle
and tore it off. Then her golden hair shone forth,
and she stood there in full splendor, and could
no longer hide herself.

—Brothers Grimm, "Allerleirauh"

4.1 MOTIVATION

In the first half of this book we studied countermeasures against a *passive*
attack, the remedy being encipherment in order to make the message unintelligible to outsiders. Now we shall deal with the *active* attack, a subject
that recently has attracted much attention. Obviously, if our bad guy Mr. X
has the power to alter data either to gain an advantage or simply to inflict
damage, the consequences are very serious indeed (see Figure 4.1).

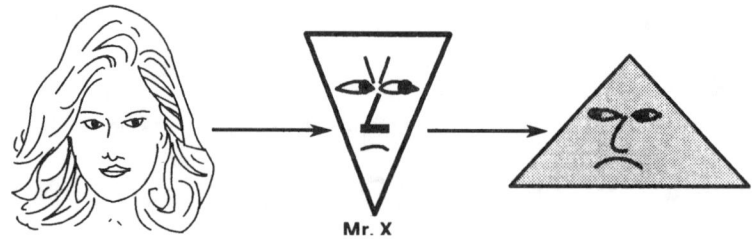

FIGURE 4.1
The active attacker

In fact, most of today's applications of cryptology ask for authentic data rather than secret data. It is convenient to distinguish the different types of problems arising from the various forms of active attacks. The appropriate security architecture for each is described by the International Standards Organization (ISO) in their *Security Addendum to the ISO reference model* [ISO].

One type of problem is concerned with the question of whether the message itself has been transmitted without alteration; this is the quest for *message integrity* (see Figure 4.2).

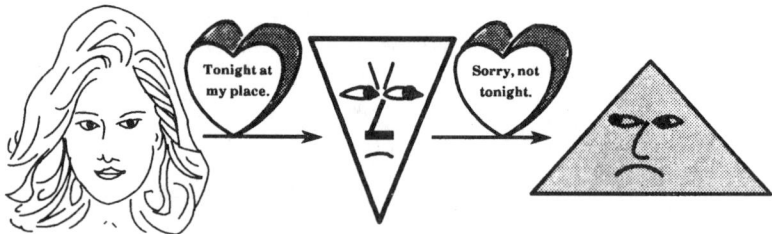

FIGURE 4.2
Message integrity

Whenever it is possible for Mr. X to alter a message, the only hope for the recipient is to become aware of any changes. So, the question becomes: Can tools be provided that enable the recipient to decide whether or not the message has been changed?

The second type of problem is similar to the first, but emphasizes the question of how the recipient can be sure that a message actually came from the sender he believes it came from. From the sender's point of view the question is whether she can later prove convincingly that she did not send the message. This is the problem of *message authentication*, also called *proof of data origin* (see Figure 4.3). In this case, the problem is to develop tools that provide the recipient with proof that the message originated from the the person who is supposed to have sent it.

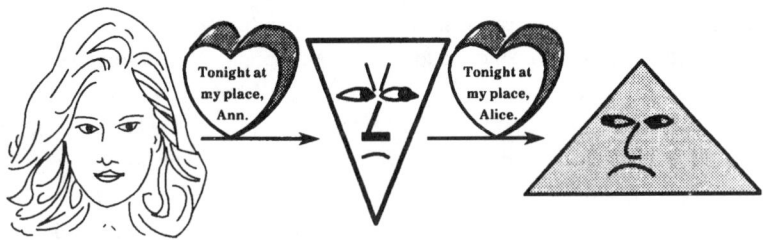

FIGURE 4.3
Message authenticity

Finally, the problem of *user authenticity* is concerned with the question of how a person can prove her (or his) identity. The recipient of a message would like to convince himself that he is talking to the person he thinks he is talking to (see Figure 4.4).

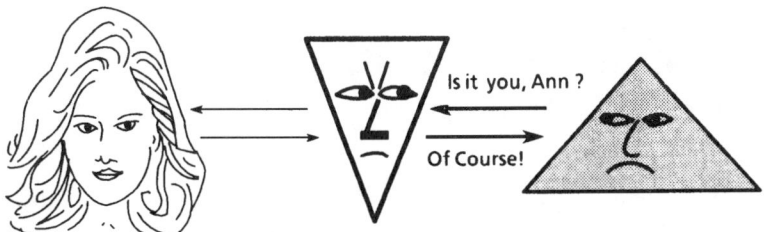

FIGURE 4.4
User authenticity

In this chapter we present several methods of solving these problems. In section 4.3 we deal with so-called *smart cards*—a new medium that helps very much to ensure integrity and authenticity.

But let us first illustrate more mundane solutions to such problems.

Once there was a lad and a lass who became friends from afar, long before they had ever met in person. After letters had been exchanged for years, finally the time came to arrange a rendezvous. Being most discreet they had never exchanged photos, so neither knew what the other looked like. How could they recognize one another? Well, they agreed upon identification signs: He carried a bouquet of flowers (not very original), while she—believe it or not—chose to carry a math book. Their meeting went without a hitch and, I am pleased to report, it was love at first sight.

Their letters have since taken on a much greater sensitivity. The two are aware, of course, that the world is full of hostile people who want to ruin their happiness. How can he be sure that the sweet messages he receives are those that she has created with such love and devotion? Simply enough; she places on the letter a drop of the perfume he knows quite intimately. What can she do to prevent the envious from altering the contents of the letter? Well, she writes with a fountain pen and, more importantly, her exquisite handwriting is virtually impossible to imitate.

In this little story we find techniques for achieving user authenticity (secret signs), message authenticity (perfume) and message integrity (ink and handwriting).

Well, so much for fiction; now let's look at the real stuff.

4.2 HOW TO ACHIEVE INTEGRITY AND AUTHENTICITY

MAC 'n Data. Remember that the aim for message integrity and authenticity is to provide a tool enabling a recipient to decide whether a received message is unchanged and authentic. In order to do this, the recipient needs something he can check the received message against. He must have additional information provided by the sender. Such information is called a *cryptographic checksum* or a *message authentication code (MAC)*; we shall use the latter term. The protocol for generating and verifying a MAC is described in Figure 4.5.

This protocol is based on a secret key k shared by the sender and the recipient, and is performed using a cryptographic algorithm A that we

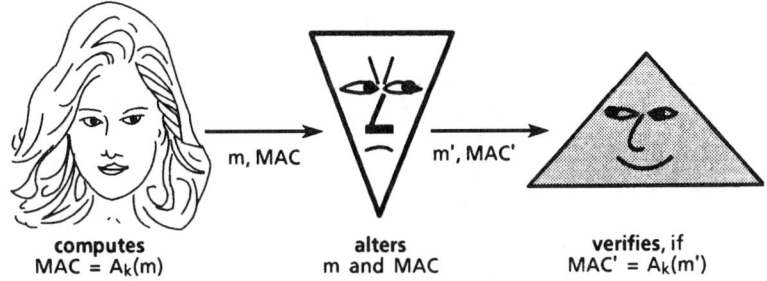

computes
MAC = $A_k(m)$

alters
m and MAC

verifies, if
MAC' = $A_k(m')$

FIGURE 4.5
MAC generation and verification

presently discuss. The sender sends not only the bare message m, but follows m with the corresponding MAC; the latter is computed from A with the secret key k, as follows.

$$MAC = A_k(m)$$

Note that m can be sent uncoded, since our present aim is not secrecy; if the sender wants in addition that the message be transmitted secretly, then he can encipher m and its MAC. The system does not prevent Mr. X from altering m and its MAC to m' and MAC$'$.

Now it's the recipient's turn to act. He very much wants to know whether the message received is the one that was sent. In order to check this, he simulates the sender's procedure. In other words, he applies the algorithm A with the key k to the received message m' and verifies whether the result coincides with the received message authentication code MAC$'$.

If $A_k(m') \neq$ MAC$'$, the recipient knows for certain that "something has happened," and he consequently does not trust the message and will reject it. If, however, $A_k(m') =$ MAC$'$ then he is reasonably certain that the message was not changed. Of course, this certainty relies heavily on the strength of the algorithm A and the number of possible keys. Let's keep in mind the underlying philosophy:

- Mr. X's deception is foiled since he must find the corresponding MAC for his message, which he cannot do since he does not know the key.

- The recipient can only detect whether the message has been altered, he has no way to recover the original of an altered message. Thus, if the verification fails, he has to ask that the message be resent.

- The mechanism of the MAC is a tool for achieving message integrity and message authenticity. We have already explained that integrity is achieved. If the verification works, then the recipient knows also that the message is authentic, since the sender is the only other person who knows the key.

A question: What kind of algorithms can one use for A in the computation of the MAC? Our first answer: Simply use any enciphering algorithm, the MAC being the ciphertext corresponding to the cleartext m. We illustrate this in Figure 4.6 with a Vigenère cipher. Apart from the use of a weak algorithm, this proposal has the disadvantage that the transmission is as twice as long as the actual message. Clearly, adding a MAC necessarily increases the amount of data that is sent, but one would like to keep this extra amount within reasonable limits.

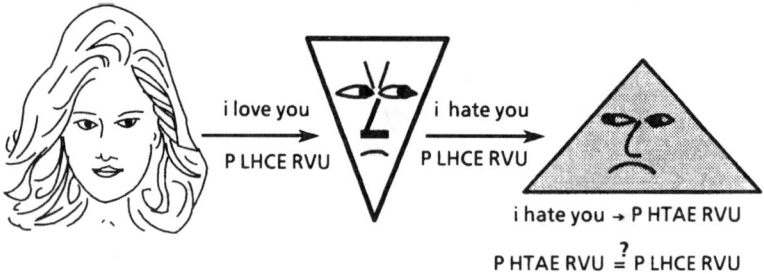

FIGURE 4.6
A simple MAC algorithm

Now we shall describe how a MAC is computed in practice. An enciphering algorithm is used, but not directly; rather, the so-called *cipher-block chaining mode* is exploited.

Suppose we have an enciphering algorithm f that transforms a block of n symbols under a fixed key k onto a ciphertext block of the same length n. A typical figure is $n = 64$ bits. In order to compute the MAC, the message m is split into blocks $m_1, m_2, \ldots, m_s$, say, each of length n. The algorithm f is then applied to m_1, yielding ciphertext c_1. Before f is applied to m_2, c_1 is added to m_2; hence one computes $c_2 = f_k(c_1 \oplus m_2)$. (Here, $\oplus$ represents addition modulo 2; that is, the first bit of c_1 is added to the first bit of m_2 obeying the rule $1 \oplus 1 = 0$. Then the second bits are added, and so on.) In the third step $c_3 = f_k(c_2 \oplus m_3)$ is computed, and so on (see Figure 4.7).

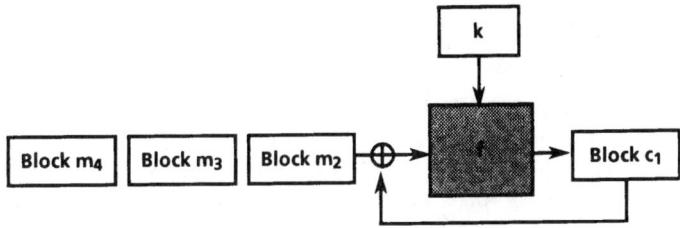

FIGURE 4.7
Generation of a MAC using the cipher-block chaining mode

The final outcome $c_s = f_k(c_{s-1} \oplus m_s)$ is then taken as the MAC. This MAC has the following properties:

- The MAC has fixed length n independent of the length of the message.
- The MAC depends on all blocks of the message.

Of course, since the messages are hashed to MACs of a fixed small length, many messages could yield the same MAC. This is not a problem for the recipient, since he has no need to recover the message from the MAC.

An arbitrarily chosen algorithm would not be effective in foiling Mr. X. To be precise, the algorithm A should have the following properties:

- It should be impossible, for all practical purposes, to obtain a message from its MAC. When this property holds the algorithm is termed a *one-way hash function*.
- It should be impossible, for all practical purposes, to find distinct messages m and m' with the same MAC. (A one-way hash function satisfying this condition is said to be *collision-free*.)

The DES algorithm mentioned in chapter 1 has proved to be satisfactory in this context, and is widely used for computing MACs.

User Authenticity.   The ability to reliably identify human beings has always been of great importance. Whereas this was formerly a process occurring between two people, today's needs have extended the process so that it must be conducted between a person and a computer. Of course, this has caused problems; however, we shall see that computers sometimes provide an effective means of user authentication. But first let us recall how this process takes place in a person-to-person communication. Identification can be based on three things:

- People can be identified by their *attributes*.
- People can be identified by their *possessions*.
- People can be identified by their *knowledge*.

The first mechanism is used repeatedly, and daily: a person can be recognized by looks, by voice, by stride, and so on. For more serious purposes fingerprints will distinguish him. The other two mechanisms are traditionally reserved for special occasions. To cash a check, identification papers are usually required—perhaps a driver's license will do; if one pays by credit card, identity is proved by the possession of the card; to cross the border into another country a passport comes in handy; and so forth. Identification by knowledge is less common—although the idea has been around from the earliest of times (see, for example, Judges 12:6). Soldiers must know the current password to gain access to a restricted area. As another example, if the police want to know whether a kidnapped person is still alive, they might ask questions that only that person could answer.

With computers the situation is quite different. Authentication by knowledge is the simplest method, and authentication by possessions is also possible; by contrast, authentication by the physical attributes of a user is quite complicated and is practical only for high-security applications. So we will deal primarily with methods of authentication based on knowledge or possession. In contrast with the third method, these methods are characterized by the fact that one participant has a secret that other participants want to be convinced he has.

Passwords. The classical method of authenticating a person by means of a machine is the use of a password. This is an arbitrarily chosen sequence of symbols (usually letters and digits), that, in theory, is known only by the person and the authenticating device. In other words, in an ideal situation—which is found rather rarely in real life—only the authentication computer and the user know the secret.

The basic idea involved in the use of a password is simple. To wit, a computer has stored in its memory a reference password P_0 that is known by the user. If the user wants to authenticate himself (for instance, in order to get access to the computer), she enters the password P, and the computer checks whether P and P_0 coincide. He gets access if $P = P_0$ (see Figure 4.8).

There are many problems involved with the improper use of passwords. We shall, however, deal with only those problems that can be solved by

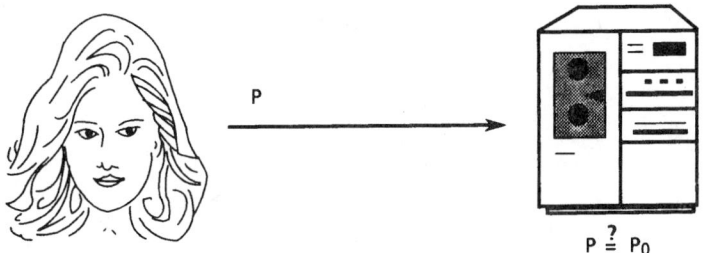

FIGURE 4.8
A simple password procedure

cryptographic means. These are primarily problems regarding the storage of passwords.

If Mr. X has (or gets) reading access to a computer's password file, he gets hold of all its passwords—and can therefore impersonate any of the computer's users. So the aforementioned procedure is secure only if the password file is kept secret—which is virtually impossible. The alert reader will already have anticipated one remedy: *encipher the passwords*. If this is done naively, the protocol proceeds as depicted in Figure 4.9. The enciphered passwords $P^* = f_k(P_0)$ are stored in the computer's memory. In the authentication process, P^* is first deciphered and then compared with the password that has been entered.

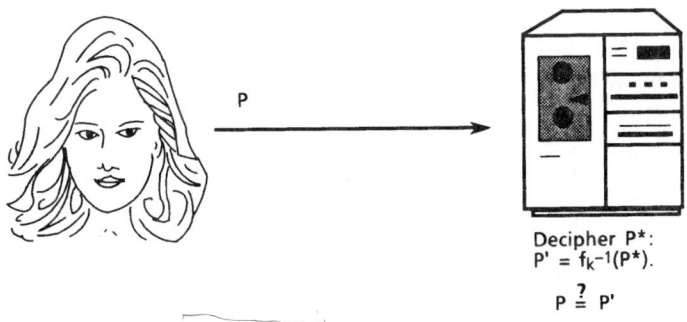

Decipher P^*:
$P' = f_k^{-1}(P^*)$.

$P \overset{?}{=} P'$

FIGURE 4.9
A password procedure that uses encipherment

The advantage of this procedure is obvious. Even if Mr. X can read the password file, he can read the enciphered passwords only (which he cannot decipher), and so he cannot simulate users by entering their respective passwords.

Is this argument correct? Well, clearly this procedure reduces the secret data quite considerably; instead of a variable number of passwords, one has only to store secretly the key k. This undoubtedly constitutes noteworthy progress, but not a solution to the problem. If Mr. X gets hold of the key, he can decipher all passwords and is again free to act as he wishes. (Ask a computer scientist how difficult it is to read data stored in software.)

After such an analysis, perhaps, the designer of a password system will not dare dream of a function that enciphers passwords without using a secret key. This sounds impossible, yet it is not. For such a job, the designer needs *one-way functions*. These are functions that map cleartexts onto ciphertexts, yet cannot be inverted. In other words, a one-way function is an invertible function with the unbelievable property that it is virtually impossible to compute the preimage of any of its resulting ciphertexts.

Although you might not realize it, the world is full of one-way functions (see exercises 2, 3, and 4). In fact, functions having time as a variable provide obvious examples. Many processes—the destruction of something by fire, for example—are easily performed in one direction but are much more difficult to reverse. (You've no doubt noticed that everyone around you is getting older and not younger.)

It's somewhat harder to invent mathematical one-way functions. Here is one: Start with any enciphering function F that maps a cleartext m onto the ciphertext $c = F_k(m)$. We shall now alter this function in a subtle way. Fix some nonsecret text m_0, which is to be fed into the algorithm not as variable cleartext, but in place of the cleartext. Next, feed a variable cleartext m into the algorithm at the position of the key. In other words, we consider the transformation

$$f : m \rightarrow c = F_m(m_0).$$

We claim that f is a one-way function. Mr. X knows m_0 and c, and wants to find m. In terms of the enciphering function F, he knows a corresponding plaintext-ciphertext pair (m_0, c) and wants to know the key m. If the algorithm F is any good, it must be resistant against this known plaintext attack, so that f is indeed a one-way function.

A question: Can one mathematically *prove* that a particular function is one-way? The answer is no! What's even worse, mathematicians have yet to find *any* function that can be proved, beyond a shadow of a doubt, to have that property. More precisely, no one knows of any function whose values can be computed in polynomial time (computed easily by a computer), but that requires exponential time (not computable by any computer) for the inverse computation. In plainer English, *certainty* is well beyond the current state of the art (see [BDG88], chapter 3, for more details). On the other hand, the functions discussed above have enough one-way properties for all practical purposes.

Now we are ready to use a "one-way" function f for password encryption. Here f can be any one-way function, not just the previous example. The value $P\# = f(P_0)$ is stored in the computer's memory. During an authentication check, f is applied to the password P, then the computer checks whether $f(P) = P\#$ (see Figure 4.10).

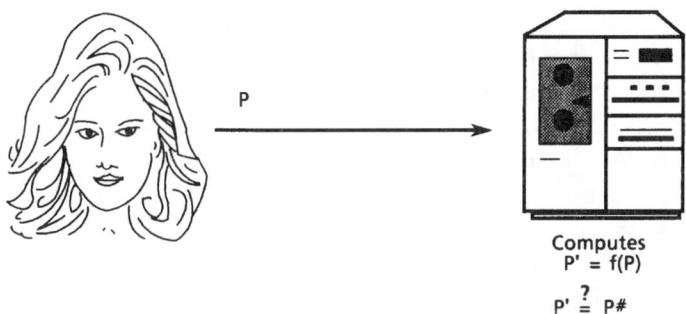

Computes
P' = f(P)

$$P' \overset{?}{=} P\#$$

FIGURE 4.10
A password procedure that uses a one-way function

The advantage of such a procedure is obvious. No one can decipher the password file and there is no secrecy involved. It is worth noting that one-way functions were invented precisely for the purpose of storing passwords secretly. In the sixties, Roger Needham from Cambridge University designed and realized such a system (see [Dif88]).

Note: This procedure, of course, cannot protect against badly chosen passwords. In fact, Mr. X can perform a kind of "chosen password" attack: If he has a list of popular passwords (first names, telephone numbers, and so on), he can apply f to these popular passwords and check whether any of the outcomes occur in the computer's password file. If so, he can impersonate the user who corresponds to that password. Empirical evidence suggests that Mr. X in this way can acquire a considerable percentage of passwords—but not of yours, since you have cleverly chosen a sophisticated, difficult-to-guess password!

Authentication Using Cards. Under strict security considerations, any password system is imperfect, one reason being that our brains are not well designed for passwords. In order to be memorized, passwords generally must be short and simple. Also, they are a *static* means of authentication. Of course, a computer may force a user to change his password every month or so, but this is only a minor improvement, since the same password is still used several times. Why is this a problem? If Mr. X listens once to the transmission of your password, he knows it, and can henceforth masquerade as you.

In order to cope with this problem the exchanges between computer and user should vary continually—a new question and a new answer each time. Of course, the user's answer must be constructed in such a way that no one else can give it. Thus, the user must perform a transformation in which a secret is involved; otherwise, Mr. X could give the answer. Such a *challenge-and-response* protocol based on secret keys is depicted in Figure 4.11. Both computer and user have a one-way function f and a common secret key k. User A sends her identification data (for instance, her name) to the computer, which then must get the key k corresponding to this data. (The key may be stored in a list, computed from the system's master key, or obtained by a similar procedure.)

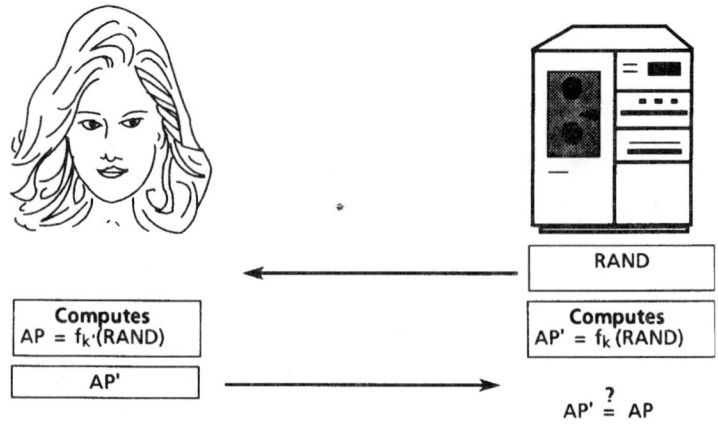

RAND

| **Computes** |
| AP $= f_{k'}$(RAND) |

| **Computes** |
| AP' $= f_k$ (RAND) |

AP'

$$AP' \stackrel{?}{=} AP$$

FIGURE 4.11
The challenge-and-response protocol

The computer must ascertain that the user who wishes to authenticate herself is in fact user A—and not, for instance, Mr. X. If the user can convince the computer that she has the right key k, then she is considered authentic. The aim of the computer in the protocol subsequently described is to determine *indirectly* that the user has the key k. In the description of the protocol we denote the user's key by k'; therefore, the computer must verify whether $k' = k$.

In order to do this the computer challenges the user by sending her a randomly chosen number $RAND$, which she cannot foretell any better than Mr. X could. She then computes the authentication parameter $AP' = f'_k(RAND)$. Simultaneously, the computer computes $AP = f_k(RAND)$ using the key k, and checks whether $AP' = AP$. If not, something went wrong; otherwise, with very high probability, the user did use the same key as the computer, and she is accepted.

There are two advantages and two disadvantages to such a procedure. First, let's examine the advantages. Since $RAND$ is chosen randomly, it continually changes, and Mr. X has no possibility whatsoever of predicting the next $RAND$. Also, AP has the character of a random number, hence Mr. X cannot give the correct response to the challenge. Equally important is the fact that although the protocol basically verifies the equality of the keys, the keys themselves are never transmitted during the protocol.

The disadvantages are small, but may not be neglected, for either theoretical or practical purposes. Observe that the computer must possess the secret keys of the users. So the computer could masquerade as the user against other instances or against itself. In other words, this protocol works only as long as the user can trust the integrity of the computer. At first glance it seems impossible to overcome this problem. We shall, however, see solutions in section 4.2.3 as well as in chapter 5.

The second disadvantage is that the user has to perform the algorithm. Certainly, women can do many things that men can only dream of, but performing a complex cryptographic algorithm should really be left to machines. Thus, f is better performed by an electronic device; one example, the smart card, will be examined in section 4.3. Consequently, a better picture of what is going on can be found in Figure 4.12.

Great, that's what computers are good for: namely, computing. Is there a problem? Yes—how does the smart card (or whatever) know that it belongs to the user? Or, more precisely: How can the smart card be sure that at this very moment its authentic owner (and not Mr. X, who might have stolen

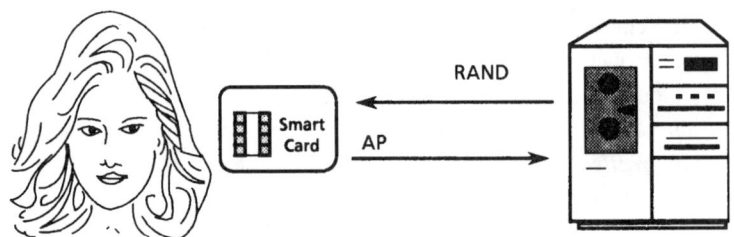

FIGURE 4.12
Challenge and response using a smart card

the card) is making use of it? Answer: The smart card requires the user to authenticate himself to the card. (See section 4.3 for more on this subject.)

Zero-Knowledge Protocols. Let me start with a personal story. Once, when I came home from work, I asked my daughter Maria, "Did you do your homework?" She promptly replied, "Of course, but I won't show it to you!" Answering my obvious question, she said, "Don't worry, everything is correct!" "This is not my problem," I had to admit, "I just wanted to convince myself that you had done your homework." But then, of course, she got angry: "I will not reveal my homework to you. You simply have to believe that I have done it!" And of course, I had to.

This seems to represent an insuperable deadlock. Maria cannot possibly convince me that she has a secret without revealing it—or can she? That is the question—and the answer is yes! It's hard to believe, but procedures exist that enable Maria (or her electronic domestics) to convince me that she has a secret without giving me the faintest idea of what the secret is. Such procedures are naturally enough called *zero-knowledge protocols*.

I will begin to demonstrate the existence of zero-knowledge protocols by presenting two examples—one being of a historical nature; the other, a game leading to the main application.

Historical Example: Tartaglia's Secret. The solution of equations has been an important activity throughout the history of mathematics. It has long been known how to solve linear equations of the sort $3x + 5 = 7$, which has the solution $x = 2/3$. (I shall use modern notation throughout.) During the Middle Ages came the solution of quadratic equations. As early as the first half of the ninth century the famous Arabian mathematician Muhammad ibn Musa Al-Khwarizmi described (in his book *Hisab al-jabr w' al-umqabala*) the solution that you have probably known since childhood. The equation $ax^2 + bx + c = 0$, for instance, has the solutions

$$x = \frac{-b \pm \sqrt{(b^2 - 4ac)}}{2a}.$$

Solving a cubic equation (that is, an equation in which x appears raised to the third power) is a lot trickier, and the solution took much longer to discover. I shall describe here only one chapter of that long story. The Venetian "reckon master" Niccolò Tartaglia ("the stammerer," ca. 1499–1557) discovered the method for solving the cubic equation $ax^3 + bx^2 + cx + d = 0$ — according to him—in 1535. He exhibited the results in a public demonstration, but kept the formula by which he had obtained them absolutely secret. But, in contrast to my deadlock situation with Maria, people could convince themselves that Tartaglia had what he claimed. They simply challenged Tartaglia by giving him a cubic equation. After a while, Tartaglia came up with a solution (that is, with the three roots of the equation)—and people could check that the solution was correct.

If, for instance, someone had submitted the equation

$$x^3 + \tfrac{1}{2} \cdot x^2 - \tfrac{13}{2} \cdot x + 3 = 0,$$

Tartaglia would have answered by giving the three roots 2, -3, and $1/2$, and anyone could convince himself that this was correct simply by checking that

$$(x - 2) \cdot (x + 3) \cdot (x - \tfrac{1}{2}) = x^3 + \tfrac{1}{2} \cdot x^2 - \tfrac{13}{2} \cdot x + 3.$$

Despite great efforts, others were unable to reproduce Tartaglia's formula.

Finally, Geronimo Cardano (1501–1576) persuaded poor Tartaglia to give him the formula, swearing to keep it secret. But, in his book *Ars Magna*, published in 1545, Cardano published Tartaglia's formula (giving credit, however, to Tartaglia). Nevertheless, it is one of those delightful ironies of history that the solution to the cubic equation goes by the name Cardano's formula.

Of course, there is more to this sordid tale. The reader should investigate this "extraordinary and bizzare" true story in [Dun90], [Eve80], [Str56], or some other history of mathematics.

What is relevant for us is the remarkable fact that Tartaglia, having a secret (how to solve cubic equations), could keep his secret and at the same time convince other people that he had it.

Example for Fun: The Square Root Game. I know a number s whose square mod 55 is 34—and you don't! I'd like to convince you that I know it without spoiling your fun in exercise 5, so I pick a random number r and square it mod 55 getting $r^2 \bmod 55 = 26$, and send you this number.

Now it's your turn. You flip a coin and if it's heads you say you want the value of $r \cdot s \bmod 55$; if tails you want only the value of r.

Suppose it's heads—then I say $r \cdot s \bmod 55 = 53$ and you can easily check that indeed

$$53^2 \bmod 55 = 4 = (26 \cdot 34) \bmod 55 = (r^2 \cdot s^2) \bmod 55$$

(see Figure 4.13). Note that it is no easier to find s knowing both $r^2 \bmod 55$ and $(r \cdot s) \bmod 55$ than it was to find s in the first place. On the other hand, it is clear that the choice of r cannot be entirely random. Among other constraints, r must exceed $\sqrt{55}$, since, should r be found from r^2, s would equal $(53/r) \bmod 55$, a very easy computation (see section 5.3.2.2 and exercise 5 in chapter 5).

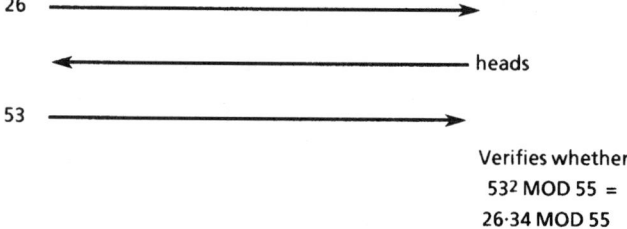

FIGURE 4.13
The Square Root Game

Let's try again. I'll tell you that $r^2 \bmod 55 = 14$. You flip and get tails, thus I'm obliged to admit that $r = 17$. Now you can easily check that indeed $17^2 = 289$ and $289 \bmod 55 = 14$.

Would I lie to you? Frankly, yes—if I thought I might get away with it. But in this game I'd *eventually* be found out. Suppose I were bluffing and didn't know s. Then I could hope that you'd ask for r (which I know, because I picked it), or else I could give you a phony $r^2 \bmod 55$ by picking a number I know to be a square mod 55, say $2^2 = 4$, and declaring my $r^2 = (4/s^2) \bmod 55 = (4/34) \bmod 55 = 26$. Now if you ask for $(r \cdot s) \bmod 55$ I simply say 2 and, lo and behold, $2^2 = 26 \cdot 34 = (4/34) \cdot 34$—all taken mod 55. (But then I wouldn't know what r could be unless I happened to know how to take square roots mod 55.)

I would get away with my bluff so long as I prepared the correct response each time, and each time I would have a 50% chance of bluffing successfully. To effectively convince you that it wasn't just a lucky guess and that I actually knew s, we'd have to repeat the process several times. Knowing s, I'd give you the right answer every time. On the other hand, if I didn't know s I'd have to anticipate your request each time. The probability of my doing that once without knowing s is $\frac{1}{2}$; twice, it's $\frac{1}{2} \cdot \frac{1}{2}$; the probability of my anticipating your request t times is $(\frac{1}{2})^t$.

Note that this is just a game, because it is fairly easy to find square roots mod 55, even by hand (see exercise 5). It does demonstrate, however, these essential features of the proper zero-knowledge protocols we will look at next:

- The protocol is interactive; both parties make random choices. (I choose the number r; you choose whether I should give you $r \cdot s$ or r.)
- The probability of my cheating and getting away with it is related to the number of times we repeat the process. The probability is cut in half each time.

Now let us look at the real thing.

The Fiat–Shamir Protocol. In 1986 two Israeli mathematicians, Adi Shamir (whom you'll meet again in chapter 5) and Amos Fiat, devised a protocol that offers a completely new dimension of user authentication. Strictly speaking, it is a computer-to-computer authentication, where one computer could be a user's smart card. This protocol [FS87] is based on the work of MIT's Shafi Goldwasser and Silvio Micali, and the University of Toronto's Charles Rackoff [GMR89]. The version discussed here is essentially the same as the square root game that was just described.

The protocol is based upon the fact that taking modular square roots of a number v—that is, finding a number whose square mod n is v—is virtually impossible when n is a number whose factorization in primes is unknown. Typically, 200-digit numbers are recommended for n; when such a number is written at normal size, it has a length of about one meter. We'll look into that problem more deeply in chapter 5. For now, knowing the modular square root of v is a very valuable secret.

Long before the process of authentication starts, a key distribution center has chosen two prime numbers p and q and formed their product $n = p \cdot q$. It is crucial that the center keep p and q secret, whereas n is public. Thus, n must be so large that Mr. X cannot factor it. The reason is that it is relatively easy to compute square roots mod p and mod q, and to compose from these numbers a square root mod n. This must be possible for the key distribution center only, not for Mr. X. (Convince yourself that the center may perform its task by solving exercises 14, 15, and 16.)

The key distribution center will present the user with a number s (which will be kept secret), the number n (a very large number), and $v = s^2 \bmod n$. The number v will serve as the user's public identification and s as her secret password. (The center may, for instance, choose as v the identification string for user A and compute s accordingly.) This is all the center is required to perform.

Figure 4.14 describes this protocol, in which the user convinces the authentication device that she knows her secret s while at the same time keeping that secret.

Several observations can be made immediately.

- Very few modulo n computations are needed. The user must square her random number to get x, and might be requested to perform $r \cdot s$. To verify the responses the authentication device must square y, and in 50% of the cases must multiply x and v.

- The authentication device uses only publicly available information, yet the secret s is employed in an essential way.

- The verifier will eventually be convinced that the user knows her secret. The probability of her cheating and getting away with it is $(1/2)^t$. With $t = 20$, that probability is less than one in one million.

- After the process, the computer has learned nothing about user A's secret.

- The security relies heavily on the fact that finding square roots modulo n is difficult, so that not even our nasty Mr. X could ever discover the secret, even after analyzing thousands of responses.

For more details see [FS87]. There are more zero-knowledge protocols; for a generalization comprising all known zero-knowledge algorithms see [BDPW90].

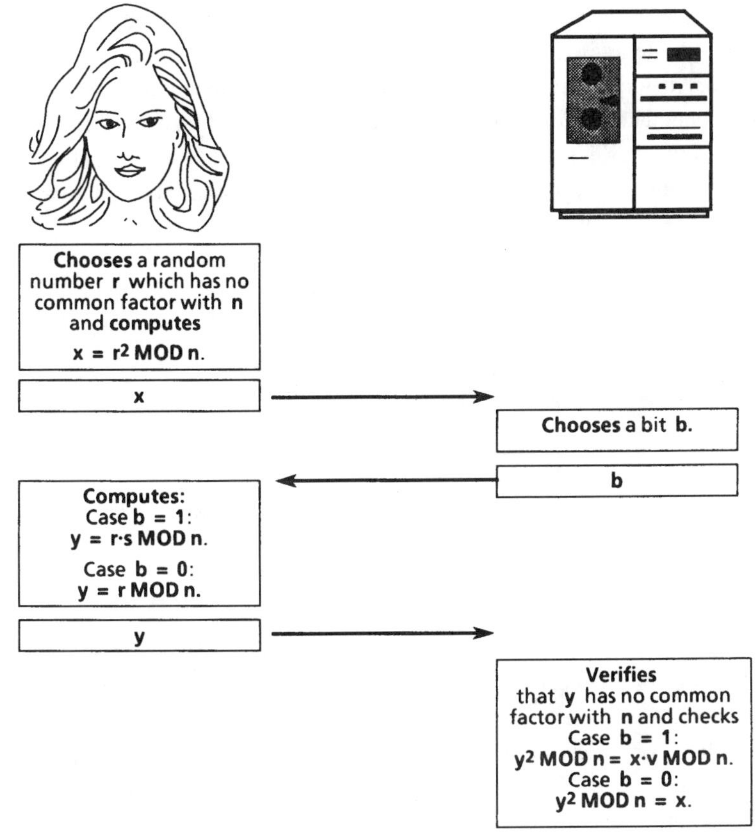
Chooses a random number r which has no common factor with n and computes
x = r2 MOD n.
x
Chooses a bit b.
b
Computes:
Case b = 1:
y = r·s MOD n.
Case b = 0:
y = r MOD n.
y
Verifies that y has no common factor with n and checks
Case b = 1:
y2 MOD n = x·v MOD n.
Case b = 0:
y2 MOD n = x.

FIGURE 4.14
The Fiat–Shamir protocol

4.3 SMART CARDS

What is a *smart card*? It is a card roughly the size of a credit card and made out of plastic, that happens to be smart. This refers to the microchip it contains that can perform calculations and store data. In other words, a smart card is a true microcomputer. It has no battery, so current must be provided externally. This is one function of the conspicuous golden contacts that distinguish a smart card from its ignorant distant cousins. Another important function of these contacts is handling the transfer of data to and from the card.

Smart cards began their evolution in 1974, when the French journalist Roland Moreno filed his patent for the "use of security features in portable memory devices." Subsequently, some hundred million smart cards have been manufactured, distributed, and used, primarily in France. Today, in all parts of the world, smart cards are used at the least in field tests, and smart cards certainly have a promising future. Today, the most widely known smart card is the Bull CP 8 card.

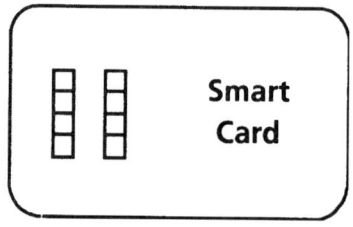

FIGURE 4.15
A smart card

Why smart cards? Or, to put it another way: Why deal with the advanced technology of smart cards in an introductory text on cryptology? The answer is simple. Smart cards, for the first time in history, provide a means for providing cryptology-based security services to the man on the street. This accomplishment can be attributed to the smart card's marriage of two features that had previously resided in opposite worlds:

- Smart cards are *ideal for cryptology*—they can perform crypto algorithms and are able to store secret keys in a secure way.
- Smart cards are *ideal for the human user*—they are extremely easy to use. As we shall see, the only burden upon the user is that he must remember his secret number in order to authenticate himself against the card.

To sum up, the smart card is no harder to use than a credit card, yet it provides an enormous amount of security and convenience. We shall discuss two typical applications of smart cards, access control and electronic shopping. For a survey of smart cards and their applications the reader is referred to [HDP90] and [McG90]; the smart card as a tool for security is studied in [BKP91].

Smart Cards for Access Control. Access control applications use smart cards as a tool between the user and the system that wants to authenticate him. The familiar old-fashioned mechanism (for instance, a password) is broken into two independent parts (see Figure 4.16).

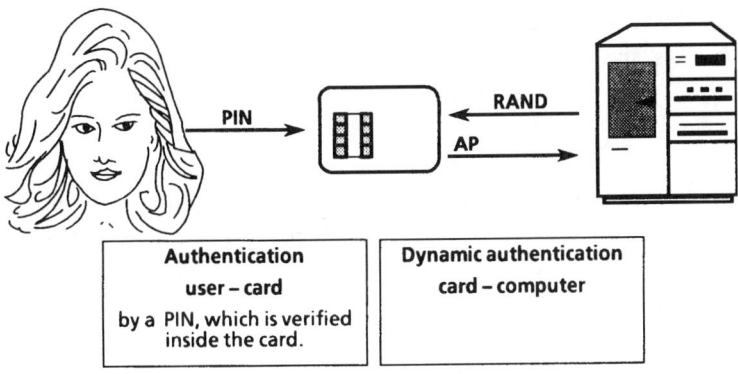

FIGURE 4.16
Two authentication protocols

- The user authenticates herself to the card by a secret number, usually called a PIN (Personal Identification Number).
- The card authenticates itself to the system by a dynamic authentication protocol.

Thus Mr. X, in order to cheat the system, has to acquire not only the user's secret number, but also her card.

Let us next consider each authentication process.

- When the user has entered her PIN using a terminal's keyboard, this number is transferred to the card and compared inside the card with a reference number. Only if these numbers coincide will the card provide any further service. (In fact, the card typically will have a mechanism that refuses further service only if there have been three consecutive unsuccessful attempts to key in the correct PIN.) Note that since the user's secret PIN is checked only by the smart card, there is no need for a central file of all secret numbers. It is conceivable that the PIN may be changed at the owner's convenience, and that it may have arbitrary length.

- The authentication of the card to the system is done using a challenge-and-response protocol as described in section 4.2.2. For this, card and central computer must have a common algorithm f and share a common secret key k. The computer challenges the card by sending it a random number $RAND$. The card applies the algorithm f under the key k to $RAND$ and sends the result AP as its response back to the computer. The latter has in the meantime also computed AP—using its key k—and can now verify whether its AP coincides with the response it has received from the card.

The advantages of such a procedure are obvious. The numbers that are exchanged vary from session to session; hence Mr. X cannot predict what the next $RAND$ or the next AP will be. Secret data (for example, keys) stay secret.

Today's smart cards have small processors and very limited memory (a few kilobytes). The reason for this is that the chip area must not exceed $20\,\mathrm{mm}^2$, or the chip will malfunction, due to the card's flexibility. As a result, only symmetric algorithms (that is, algorithms for which both sides need to know the same secret key) are used at present. It would be desirable for smart cards to perform zero-knowledge protocols (indeed, the Fiat–Shamir algorithm was designed expressly for smart cards) and public key algorithms (to be discussed in the next chapter). Such algorithms cannot be implemented with secure key length and satisfying performance, due to the limited capacity of today's smart cards (see [FP90]). But this certainly will change in the near future; better cards have already been announced.

Electronic Shopping. The idea of *electronic shopping*, also called *POS-Banking* (POS standing for point of sale), is that a customer in a store, after choosing goods, pays the whole amount neither by cash, nor check, nor credit card (where signing and paper are also required), but—most simply—using a smart card.

At first glance one might think that the customer is faced with the same old problems—in particular, that of authenticating herself to the shopkeeper. And the situation seems further complicated, since there are three parties involved: the customer, the shopkeeper, and the bank. Yet even this situation is very much simplified by the use of a smart card, particularly when the customer and shopkeeper have the same bank (see Figure 4.17).

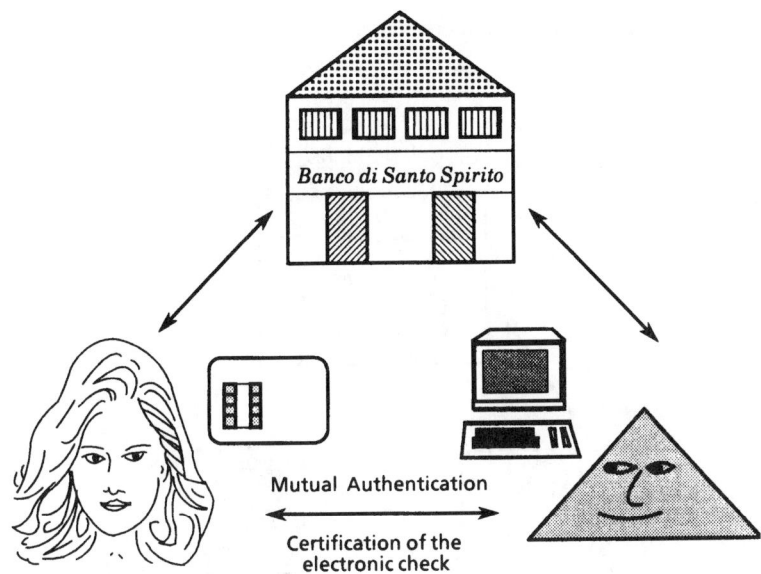

FIGURE 4.17
Electronic shopping

One should distinguish between two processes: authentication of the communication partners, and authentication of the message (which in this case is a sort of electronic check).

The authentication of the customer to the shopkeeper's terminal is performed as previously described. Typically, an authentication of the shopkeeper's terminal to the card is also desirable, since there conceivably could be fraudulent terminals. This authentication proceeds in a similar way: the card sends a random number to the terminal and verifies whether the response is correct.

A quite different problem is the authentication of the electronic check. This document is "signed" by a sort of MAC and then sent from the card to the shopkeeper's terminal. It is crucial that the shopkeeper cannot change this check. On the other hand it is desirable that the shopkeeper be able to verify the validity of the electronic check. The problem with a symmetric algorithm is that anyone who can verify the MAC is also (theoretically) able to alter the document and compute the corresponding new MAC, since he has the secret key. The use of a public key signature scheme (see chapter 5) would solve this problem elegantly.

When restricted to symmetric algorithms, authentication of an electronic check can proceed as shown in Figure 4.18.

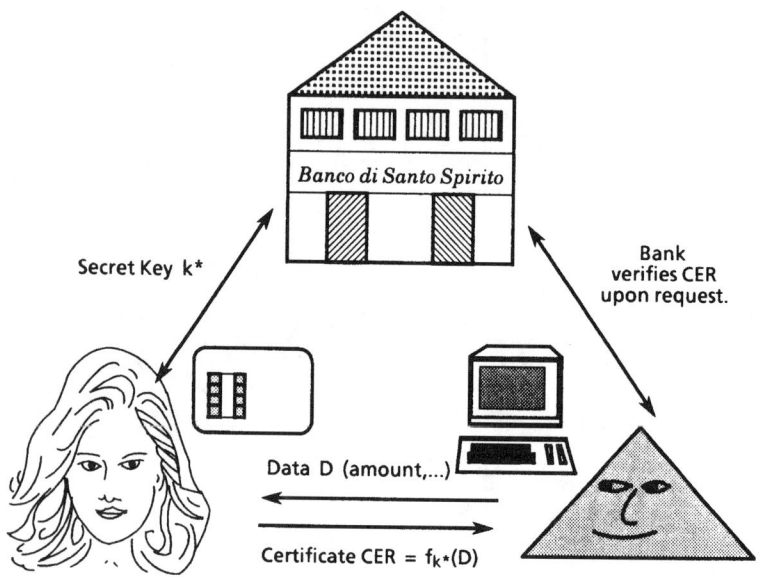

FIGURE 4.18
Certification

Customer and bank share a common secret key k^* unknown to the shopkeeper. The electronic check is then MAC'ed (as in 4.2.1) using this key k^*. When customer and card have been accepted as authentic, they can actually pay the amount. In order to accomplish this, the customer must acknowledge the data D (amount, type of goods, date, shopkeeper's name, and so forth) and send it back to the shopkeeper, such that

- the shopkeeper has a guarantee that he will get his money, and

- the shopkeeper cannot alter the data. (A crooked shopkeeper could increase the amount in order to get more money from the customer's bank.)

In order to make such a deception impossible, the card again utilizes the secret key k^*. The card not only sends back the data D, but also the data "signed" using the key k^* in order to compute the corresponding MAC. The MAC constructed in this way is sometimes called a *certificate* and denoted by CER; the whole procedure is referred to as the *certification* of the data. This CER guarantees that the shopkeeper cannot successfully alter the check. But if he wants to convince himself that the MAC actually corresponds to the electronic check, he asks the bank to verify this correspondence.

Using certificates is not an ideal solution; it has two disadvantages. Both parties, customer and shopkeeper, must trust the bank. Moreover, the shopkeeper cannot verify the electronic check instantaneously; that procedure works only upon request.

Nonetheless, it is generally believed that such systems already provide much greater security to all participants than other card-based payment systems.

EXERCISES

1. Do you associate enciphering, integrity, message authentication, or user authentication with the following notions?
   - a fingerprint
   - a seal on a document
   - a brief case with combination lock
   - the plastic seal on an unopened aspirin bottle
   - a chastity belt
   - a dessert artfully decorated with whipped cream

2. Interpret the following events as one-way functions (if possible!).
   - breaking one's leg
   - squeezing toothpaste (even better, glue) out of a tube
   - turning the playroom upside-down ("playing")
   - brainwashing
   - mixing paint
   - conceiving for the first time the relationship "$e = mc^2$"
   - dying
   - giving birth

3. Most of the actions of the preceding exercise can be described as transitions from order to chaos. Which ones cannot?

4. Does the following illustrate a one-way function? Given a name, it is easy to find the corresponding phone number in a directory. Conversely, given a phone number, it is extremely difficult to find the corresponding

name. (There is an easy way to get the corresponding name: just dial the number!)

5. Find the modular square roots of 34 modulo 55 (that is, all numbers s satisfying $s^2 \bmod 55 = 34$).

6. Who is at a disadvantage in the challenge-and-response protocol if the random number $RAND$ is in fact not chosen randomly? Distinguish between two cases:
   (a) where $RAND$ is constant;
   (b) where $RAND$ is not constant but predictable (e.g., $RAND_{new} = RAND_{old} + 1$).
   Discuss in particular whether anyone other than the challenger has a disadvantage.

7. Interpret the following story with regard to the notions of secrecy and authentication.

   In the Departement du Gard—as you rightly recall that is where Nîmes and the Pont du Gard can be found in southern France—there sat an elderly spinster who was a postal clerk with the nasty habit of opening, just a little, the letters and reading them. Every one knew it. But so it goes in France. Concierge, Telephone and Postal Service are sacrosanct institutions; you are allowed to complain about them, but you had better not, and so no one does.

   And so the lady read the letters and inflicted upon the population a certain amount of grief with her indiscretion.

   In his splendid castle in the district there lived a clever count. Counts are sometimes clever, in France. And one day this count did the following thing:

   He summoned a bailiff to the castle and wrote in his presence to a friend:

   Dear Friend!

   Since I know that the postmistress Emilie Dupont constantly opens and reads our letters, as she would explode from sheer curiosity, I enclose a live flea to expose her handiwork.

   With best wishes   *Count Koks.*

   And this letter he sealed in the presence of the Bailiff. But he enclosed no flea. When the letter was delivered, there was a flea inside.

   Kurt Tucholsky, *The Flea*

8. List at least 20 words, each consisting of at least six symbols, that shouldn't be used as passwords.

9. Consider the following simple MAC. For a message written in plain English, the MAC is the ciphertext under an additive cipher.

    (a) Show that when the evil Mr. X has substituted a text of his own, the probability that he is not detected is at least $1/26$.

    (b) Explain what happens if the text consists of at least two letters.

    (c) Is the probability of successfully cheating in general greater than $1/26$?

10. Play Mr. X's role and find out the key of the example in Figure 4.6.

11. The plot development in Shakespeare's *King Lear* depends on four important letters. Convince yourself that if the characters had read this book, the play might well have had a happy ending. In particular read the following scenes.

    Act I, scene ii. Edmund, bastard son to Gloucester, passes off as a letter from the natural son Edgar a letter he himself has written (which "exposes" the entirely invented dastardly intent of Edgar). If Gloucester understood authentication, he would dismiss the letter as a forgery!

    Act II, scene iv. Goneril's letter to sister Regan is seen by one of Lear's loyal followers as it is being delivered. The result is an argument that leads to Lear's madness. Goneril should have read about anonymity (see chapter 6).

    Act III, scene iii. A letter to Gloucester informing him that an army has gathered in support of the deposed King falls into the hands of the enemy. This shows that any system of security is doomed to fail when someone who is honest but gullible (Gloucester) puts his trust in someone who is determined and treacherous (Edmund).

    Act IV, scene vi. Edgar intercepts Goneril's letter to Edmund, the letter that suggests they do in her husband. She should have read this book and used some sort of cipher!

12. Interpret the following procedure as a zero-knowledge protocol. This particularly nice illustration is due to the families of Jean-Jaques Quisquater of Belgium and Louis Guillou of France. You should not fail to read their delightful paper [QG90].

    A story tells us about Circe and Ulysses. Circe's secret in this case consists of the knowledge necessary to open a magic door. As would any powerful sorceress, she wants to keep her secret; certainly she doesn't want to reveal it to Ulysses. For this purpose, the entrance to the building that encloses the magic door has a particularly sophisticated design (see Figure 4.19).

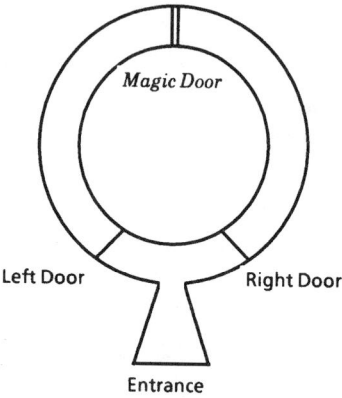

FIGURE 4.19

The Magic Door

The protocol is as follows. Circe passes through the entrance and walks either left or right, closing the corresponding door behind her. Only at this point is Ulysses allowed to enter the building (through the entrance), but he must not walk any further—thus, he cannot know the direction she has chosen. Now he chooses left or right and asks Circe to return using the door he has selected. If Circe can indeed open the magic door, she can do what Ulysses has requested; if she doesn't possess the secret knowledge, she can only succeed with probability $\frac{1}{2}$.

13. Determine which numbers can be the square of a number mod 11. (For instance 5 is a square mod 11, since $42 \bmod 11 = 5$.)

14. Convince yourself that the square root of a number mod 11 is obtained by raising this number to the third power mod 11—that is, the number y defined by

$$y := x^3 \bmod 11$$

has the property that $y^2 \bmod 11 = x$.

15. In general, the following fact is true: If p is a prime number with $p \bmod 4 = 3$, then one obtains a square root of a number $x \bmod p$ by

raising x to its $(p+1)/4$th power mod p. Try at least two prime numbers different from 11 in order to convince yourself of this fact. (If you already know that the numbers $1, 2, \ldots, p-1$ form a multiplicative cyclic group, then you are also able to prove this fact.)

16. Why did I insist on the fact that the number x in the Fiat–Shamir algorithm has no common factor with n? (Hint: Consider the case $x = 0$.)

17. What is the use of the random number r in the Fiat–Shamir protocol? (Hint: If B knew r, he could, by cleverly choosing his bit b, find out the secret s.)

18. Convince yourself that in the Fiat–Shamir protocol, Mr. X, wanting to pass himself off as the authentic user (even though he does not know the secret s), can successfully cheat in any round with probability $\frac{1}{2}$. (Hint: Assume that Mr. X knows what bit b is going to be sent. Then he first chooses y, and then x suitably in such a way that the verification process of b works.)

Chapter 5

THE FUTURE HAS ALREADY STARTED
or
PUBLIC KEY CRYPTOGRAPHY

Rain just rains down;
it just doesn't rain up.

—Bertholt Brecht

The cipher systems we have explored so far possess two properties in common:

- Anyone who can encipher a message is also able to decipher it, and

- Sender and receiver share a common secret key which must be transmitted before an encryption procedure can start.

While the second property is undoubtedly a disadvantage, one is inclined to believe that the first property (more or less the definition of the *symmetric* cipher systems that we have considered up to now) is an advantage, since it means that the same machine can be used for enciphering and deciphering. *Asymmetric* systems are defined by the negation of the first property. (I shall use the terms *public key* and *asymmetric* synonymously.) It turns out that such systems do not have the second property, rendering key management (at least theoretically) quite simple.

Such systems were first proposed by Whitfield Diffie and Martin Hellman of Stanford University in a 1976 paper entitled "New Directions in Cryptography" [DH76]—a paper that lives up to the promise of its title. Diffie, in a highly recommended survey article [Dif88], writes,

Public key cryptography was born in May 1975, the child of two problems...the key distribution problem and the problem of signatures .... The discovery consisted not of a solution, but of the recognition that the two problems, each of which seemed unsolvable by definition, could be solved at all and that the solutions to both came in one package.

5.1 PUBLIC-KEY CRYPTOSYSTEMS

We shall work under the assumption that any participant P has one pair of keys,

- a *public key* $E = E_P$ for enciphering, and
- a *private (secret) key* $D = D_P$ for deciphering,

with the property that *it is not feasible to compute D_P from E_P*. A system having this property is called a *public key cryptosystem*. At first glance it seems incredible that such systems could actually exist. Later we shall see that there are indeed successful realizations.

All public keys are publicly available; they might be stored in a public file (as in a phone book). On the other hand, the private keys are kept secret; they are known only to their owners (or, more likely, to the computers of their owners). Figure 5.1 summarizes this scenario. (We've used our artistic license to leave open the shutters, which certainly should have been kept closed to hide the secret keys.)

A public key cryptosystem is called a *public key encryption scheme*, if for any message m we have

$$D(E(m)) = m.$$

A public key cryptosystem is called a *public key signature scheme*, if for any message m one can verify using the public key E that m and $D(m)$ fit.

Here some remarks are in order.

- In our context it seems sensible to write $E(m)$ for the ciphertext obtained from a message m by using the key E. This notation differs slightly from the convention used in chapter 3.
- The defining property for a public key encryption scheme says that the ciphertext $E(m)$ will be deciphered correctly by using the key D; this property is clearly desirable for an enciphering system.

FIGURE 5.1

Private and public keys

- We have deliberately defined a public key signature scheme in a general fashion. We shall see later how the property that m, $D(m)$, and E "fit" can be made concrete.

- There are public key encryption systems, there are asymmetric signature scheme systems, and there are systems which satisfy both properties.

Let us now suppose that we have an asymmetric encryption scheme. The public and the private keys must be in place in order to start enciphering. Here is how the process works (see Figure 5.2).

1. If A wants to send the message m to B, A
   - looks up the public key E_B of B,

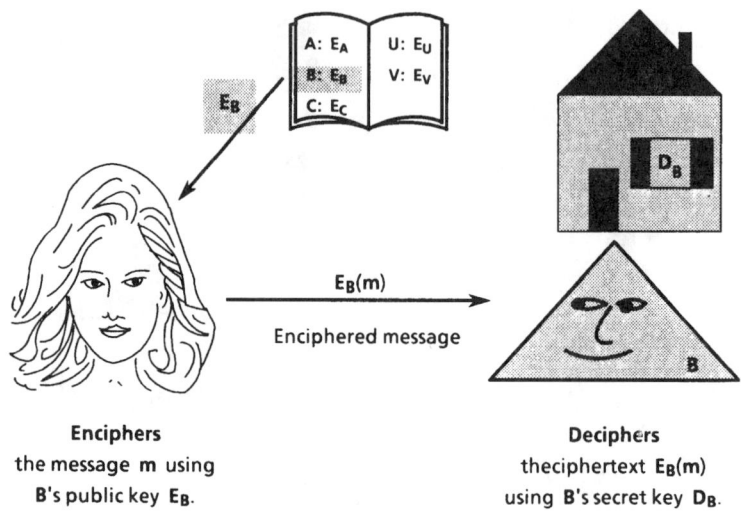

Enciphers the message **m** using B's public key **E_B**.	**Deciphers** theciphertext **E_B(m)** using B's secret key **D_B**.

FIGURE 5.2
Public key encryption scheme

- enciphers the message m using E_B, and
- sends $E_B(m)$ to B.

2. B is able to decipher the ciphertext $E_B(m)$, since he (exclusively) knows the key D_B:

$$D_B(E_B(m)) = m.$$

3. No other participant can decipher $E_B(m)$, since, by hypothesis, no one can deduce D_B from E_B (and $E_B(m)$).

Note that only keys related to the recipient B are used.

At first glance this procedure seems rather bewildering. In order that its basic simplicity (that is, its ingenuity) may be appreciated, we shall illustrate it using everyday notions. Imagine a cluster of mailboxes. Suppose that each participant of our imaginary communication system has a mailbox with his name on it, and his own private key. Applying the public key corresponds to inserting a letter into the mailbox. The individual keys for the mailboxes correspond to the secret keys (see Figure 5.3).

If someone wants to send a message to Mrs. P. Rivate, he simply puts the message into Mrs. Rivate's mailbox. (This corresponds to enciphering

FIGURE 5.3
Mailboxes

the message; now no one can see the message. Indeed, this operation is extremely easy to perform.) Note how the analogy respects the basic property of a public key cryptosystem: knowing how to deliver the message does not make the inverse any easier at all.

Now anyone, even the sender, may try his key on the mailbox—without any success! Only Mrs. Rivate may open the lock—and she may do so without any difficulty.

Let's now look again at public key cryptosystems in general. Such a system has the following noteworthy advantages.

- No key exchange among the participants is necessary.

The fundamental problem of symmetric algorithms has most elegantly and effectively been solved with one stroke. The important consequence is that public key systems offer the possibility of spontaneous communication. I am in a position to send secret messages to a colleague without any need to have previously agreed upon a secret key. One can express this fact also by saying that public key cryptosystems are ideally suited for open communications.

- One needs relatively few keys.

Using symmetric crypto systems, every pair of participants has to have an exclusive secret key; n participants need $n \cdot (n - 1)/2$ different keys. But using an asymmetric algorithm, each participant needs only two keys, and only one of these keys must be kept secret. Thus the number of keys is only double the number of participants. So, 1001 participants in a symmetric system would require 500,500 keys, compared with a mere 2002 keys for an asymmetric system.

- New participants can join the system without new problems for the old members.

If a new participant joins a symmetric cryptosystem, all the other users have to exchange a secret key with him. In this asymmetric situation, the old members do not have to update their databases.

- Public key algorithms offer an excellent possibility for digital signatures.

I discuss this at length in section 5.2.

Of course, there are also disadvantages to asymmetric algorithms; two examples follow.

- Today we know of no asymmetric algorithm which is both secure— beyond any reasonable doubt—and fast.

The asymmetric algorithm that currently leads the pack is the RSA algorithm, to be discussed in section 5.3. On the other hand, algorithms based on discrete logarithms have quite justly received much attention of late, so we shall also look at what they have to offer.

- Contrary to first impression, even public key algorithms need some key management. At first glance, everything seems to be easy. Every new participant gets a new pair of keys (or chooses his pair by himself) and he's on his way, or so you would think. What could go wrong? Well, what happens in our example if I set up a mailbox with the false name sticker "Rivate" and only my key opens it? Then everything sent to Mrs. Rivate becomes available to me.

This threat can be circumvented by using a clever kind of key management which guarantees that the public keys are authentic. This notion will be developed in exercise 15.

5.2 DIGITAL SIGNATURES

Another extremely important idea presented by Diffie and Hellman is that of a digital (or electronic) signature. First, let's recall some attributes of the usual handwritten signature. Suppose that our doctor, Dr. Adams, has signed a prescription. Then, ideally, her signature has the following characteristics.

- Only Dr. Adams may produce this signature, and
- Anyone may verify that this signature is hers.

Analogous characteristics can be achieved using an asymmetric signature scheme in the following way.

1. If Dr. Adams wants to sign a message m, then she
   - "enciphers" m with her private key D_A (which is known exclusively to her), and
   - publishes the message signed in this way $D_A(m)$ along with the message m itself.

2. Any other participant may verify the electronic signature $D_A(m)$ by using Dr. Adam's public key E_A and checking whether m and $D_A(m)$ fit (see Figure 5.4).

If the famous RSA signature scheme is applied (see section 5.3), the verification works by applying E_A to the signature $D_A(m)$ and checking whether the following equation holds.

$$E_A(D_A(m)) = m$$

In such a situation, there is sometimes another possibility for verifying the electronic signature: The signer publishes only $D_A(m)$, but not the message m. The verifier applies E_A to the signature; if the outcome yields a sensible message (giving, for instance, the details of a prescription), then this fact proves the validity of the signature. (In order to apply this procedure we must assume that m is indeed a meaningful message, and not only a random sequence of symbols; so this method could be applied for the signature of English texts.)

Every recipient can *verify* the signature, that is, prove authorship of the received document. Although it is not the case that current law recognizes such signatures, in a conflict a judge might very well base his decision on a

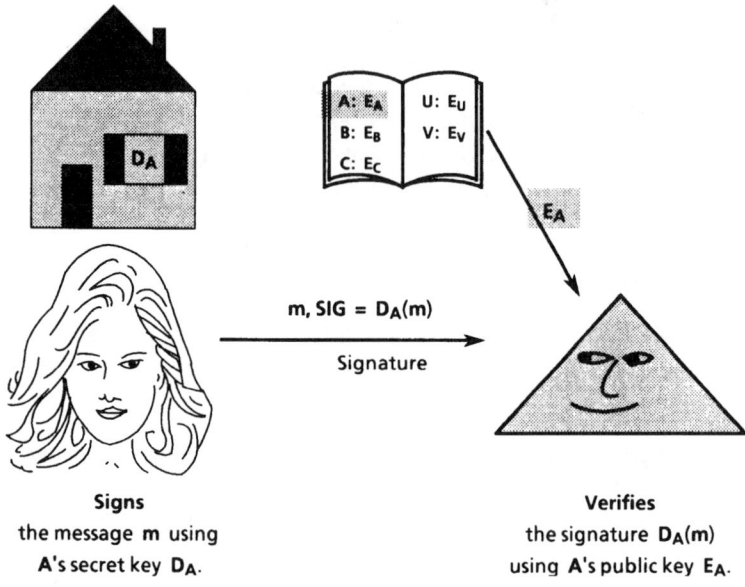

Signs
the message **m** using
A's secret key D_A.

Verifies
the signature $D_A(m)$
using A's public key E_A.

FIGURE 5.4
Public key signature scheme

digital signature. It would be rather difficult for Dr. Adams to deny having sent that message. Note that only keys related to the sender A are used.

The crucial difference from a handwritten signature is that the electronic signature $D_A(m)$ is intimately connected with the message, whereas the handwritten signature is adjoined to the message and always looks the same. As a consequence, no one can alter the signed message $D_A(m)$ without everyone being able to see that the document has been changed. For, if $D_A(m)$ is altered at all, then the application of the public key E_A to the altered signed message $D_A(m)'$ yields a cleartext which will appear totally random.

Unfortunately, we are not able to explain the principle of a digital signature with our mailbox example. The analogous mechanical system must have the property that one gets the original message back if one uses first the private and then the corresponding public key. In our example this would mean that one first removed a letter from the empty mailbox with the private key, and then inserted a letter with the public key, resulting in an empty mailbox. The analogy breaks down because the mechanical operations fail to commute. In order to remedy this deficiency we now present a peculiar lock mechanism which has the property that locking and unlocking commute. This is the "asymmetric bolt" of Peter A. Schlaube. You may admire this miracle of technology in the following picture.

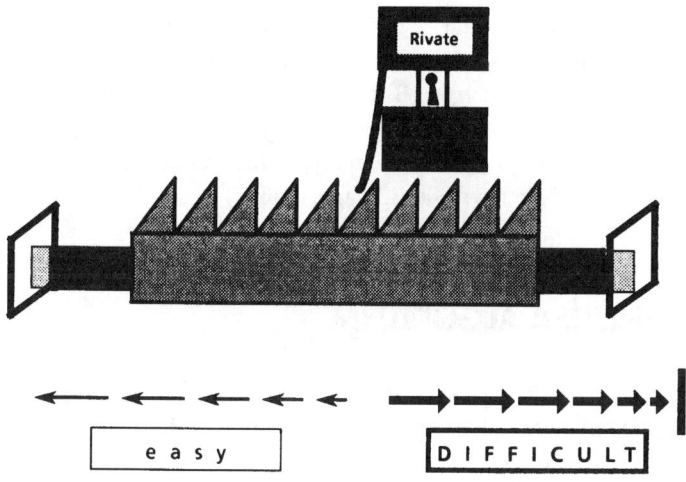

FIGURE 5.5
The asymmetric bolt

You see a bolt which slides closed in two directions; that is, it is secured when pushed to the right as well as when pushed to the left. However, without a key the bolt slides only to the left; a catch mechanism prevents the bolt from moving to the right. Only the owner (in this example Mrs. P. Rivate) may release the catch using her private key and then, without any difficulty, push the bolt to the right.

Imagine now that all mailboxes come with such an asymmetric bolt. This means that a mailbox must be opened even when putting a letter in it—and then secured by an asymmetric bolt. If Mrs. Rivate wants to sign a document, she puts the document in her mailbox, closes it by pushing the bolt to the *right* (after having released the catch), then resets the mechanism. Now anyone can verify whether this mailbox contains a signed document. This is the case if and only if the mailbox opens by pushing the bolt to the *left* (application of the public key).

You have no doubt noticed a problem with allowing anyone to verify the signature—once the signature has been verified (that is, once the bolt has been pushed to the left), no one else may verify the signature.

If Mrs. Rivate wants only Mr. P. U. Blic to be able to verify her signature, she can proceed as follows. She signs her message (that is, she puts the message into her mailbox, releases the catch, and closes her mailbox by pushing the bolt to the right). Now she enciphers her signed message using Mr. Blic's public key. That is, she puts her closed mailbox into the gigantic mailbox of Mr. Blic. Then Mr. Blic (and he alone) may decipher the signed message using his secret key. He gets thereby the signed message and may verify Mrs. Rivate's signature by applying her public key. We leave the diagram of all this to the reader's imagination.

5.3 THE RSA ALGORITHM

Certainly all this discussion of locks and bolts is fascinating, but it leaves something to be desired when it comes to securing electronically transmitted and stored data. Does there exist an actual realization of asymmetric systems?

In 1977 three people who were to make the single most spectacular contribution to public key cryptography: Ronald Rivest, Adi Shamir, and Leonard Adleman . . . took up the challenge of producing a full-fledged public-key cryptosystem. The process lasted several months during which Rivest proposed approaches, Adleman attacked them, and Shamir recalls doing some of each. In May 1977 they were rewarded with success . . . . They had discovered how a simple piece of classical number theory could be made to solve the problem. [Dif88]

In the meantime, other asymmetric algorithms have been invented and reinvented, but none of them is as well known and as intensively discussed as the RSA algorithm.

To describe this algorithm we need a little bit of mathematics, in particular a fact about numbers which is usually attributed to the Swiss mathematician Leonhard Euler (pronounced "oiler," 1707–1783). In the sequel, we shall use only the results of the following two sections, not the accompanying arguments, so you may skip most parts of 5.3.1 and 5.3.2. If subsequently you want to know more about the details, you may of course return to the relevant passages.

A Theorem of Euler. The RSA algorithm is a direct application of Euler's theorem. Before stating the theorem, we will first make several definitions and assertions.

For a natural number n we define $\phi(n)$ to be the number of positive integers smaller than or equal to n that have no factor except 1 in common with n. In other words, we search for all positive integers smaller than n that are relatively prime to n—their greatest common divisor with n equals 1. This sounds more complicated than it actually is. Some examples may clarify this.

$$\phi(1) = 1, \ \phi(2) = 1, \ \phi(3) = 2, \ \phi(4) = 2,$$

$$\phi(6) = 2, \ \phi(10) = 4, \ \phi(15) = 8.$$

(The last assertion can be seen as follows. The positive integers < 15 that are relatively prime to 15 are 1, 2, 4, 7, 8, 11, 13 and 14. Since these are 8 different numbers, we have $\phi(15) = 8$.)

We can demonstrate the validity of the following claims regarding our definition.

1. *If p denotes a prime number, then*

$$\phi(p) = p - 1,$$

because all the $p - 1$ integers $1, 2, 3, \ldots, p - 1$ are relatively prime to p.

2. *If p and q are two distinct primes, then*

$$\phi(pq) = (p - 1)(q - 1).$$

There is a total of $pq - 1$ positive integers smaller than pq. We count how many of them are not relatively prime to pq. On the one hand, these are the $q - 1$ multiples of p, namely

$$p, 2p, 3p, \ldots, (q - 1)p,$$

and on the other hand the $p - 1$ multiples

$$q, 2q, 3q, \ldots, (p - 1)q$$

of q. Since these are the only integers between 1 and $pq - 1$ that are *not* relatively prime to pq, it follows that

$$\phi(pq) = pq - 1 - (q - 1) - (p - 1) = pq - q - p + 1 = (p - 1)(q - 1).$$

Now we are able to formulate the Theorem of Euler:

Denote by m and n two relatively prime positive integers. Then

$$m^{\phi(n)} \bmod n = 1.$$

We shall be particularly interested in the case when n is the product of two distinct primes. In view of the second claim, Euler's theorem reads as follows.

Let m be an integer that has no common factor except 1 with either of the two distinct primes p and q. Then

$$m^{(p-1)(q-1)} \bmod pq = 1.$$

In other words, if the large number $m^{(p-1)(q-1)}$ is divided by pq, it leaves 1 as its remainder.

We won't spend time proving this (not too difficult) theorem. (For a proof see, for instance, [HW60]; see also Exercises 12, 13, and 14.) However, one should consider a couple of examples. The assertion

$$5^{\phi(6)} \bmod 6 = 5^2 \bmod 6 = 25 \bmod 6 = 1$$

can easily be checked. To verify that

$$31^{792} \bmod 851 = 31^{22 \cdot 36} \bmod 851$$

$$= 31^{\phi(23 \cdot 37)} \bmod 851 = 31^{\phi(851)} \bmod 851 = 1$$

would require considerably more effort.

The Euclidean Algorithm.   The Euclidean algorithm will be used to produce the private and public key of any participant. The objective of the Euclidean algorithm is to compute the greatest common divisor $\gcd(a, b)$ of two given positive integers a and b ($a \geq b$). Perhaps you think that computing $\gcd(a, b)$ is the same as factoring; so, for example, $24 = 2 \cdot 2 \cdot 2 \cdot 3$ and

$18 = 2 \cdot 3 \cdot 3$ imply that $\gcd(24, 18) = 2 \cdot 3 = 6$. At first glance (with small numbers) the method seems infallible. However, during this chapter we will observe the following two facts.

- It is extremely difficult to factor a large number.
- Nevertheless, using the Euclidean algorithm it is extremely simple to calculate the gcd of two (even very large) numbers.

We will first deal with the second claim.

Computing the gcd. We shall start with an example. Let $a = 792$ and $b = 75$.

$$792 = 10 \cdot 75 + 42$$
$$75 = 1 \cdot 42 + 33$$
$$42 = 1 \cdot 33 + 9$$
$$33 = 3 \cdot 9 + 6$$
$$9 = 1 \cdot 6 + 3$$
$$6 = 2 \cdot 3$$

My claim is that 3 is the greatest common divisor of 792 and 75. Its proof comes from considering the general scheme, as follows.

Euclidean algorithm.

$$r_0 = a$$
$$r_1 = b$$
$$r_0 = q_1 \cdot r_1 + r_2 \qquad 0 < r_2 < r_1$$
$$r_1 = q_2 \cdot r_2 + r_3 \qquad 0 < r_3 < r_2$$
$$\vdots \qquad\qquad \vdots$$
$$r_{i-1} = q_i \cdot r_i + r_{i+1} \qquad 0 < r_{i+1} < r_i$$
$$\vdots \qquad\qquad \vdots$$
$$r_{n-2} = q_{n-1} \cdot r_{n-1} + r_n \qquad 0 < r_n < r_{n-1}$$
$$r_{n-1} = q_n \cdot r_n.$$

We claim that the number r_n defined by the Euclidean algorithm is the greatest common divisor of a and b. In order to see this, we must demonstrate the following assertions.

- r_n divides a and b (that is, r_n is a common divisor), and
- any number z that divides a and b divides also r_n (that is, r_n is the greatest among all common divisors).

In order to prove the first step we must consider the above system of equations from toe to top.

Since $r_{n-1} = q_n \cdot r_n$, r_n is a divisor of r_{n-1}.
Hence r_n divides $q_{n-1} \cdot r_{n-1} + r_n$ and hence r_{n-2}.
$$\vdots$$
Therefore, r_n divides r_i (and r_{i+1}) and hence r_{i-1}.

Finally we get that r_n divides the numbers $r_1 (= b)$ and $r_0 (= a)$. Hence, r_n is in fact a common divisor of a and b.

In order to prove step two, one must pass through the equations top-down. We will skip this; the reader is referred to exercise 3.

For computer enthusiasts (and in order to be prepared for exercise 4) we will describe the Euclidean algorithm in a sort of pidgin programming language.

```
Read a, b
While b ≠ 0 do
    r := a mod b
    a := b, b := r
Write a.
```

One advantage of this description is that there are no ugly and disagreeable indices.

Computing the modular inverse of an integer.   For our purposes the following assertion is of the utmost importance.

Given positive integers a and b with $d = gcd(a, b)$, then there are integers x and y with the property that

$$d = xa + yb.$$

In order to compute x and y we have to inspect the equations of the Euclidean algorithm a last time (I promise). We get successively

$$d = r_n = r_{n-2} - q_{n-1} \cdot r_{n-1} = r_{n-2} + (-q_{n-1}) \cdot r_{n-1}$$

$$= r_{n-2} - q_{n-1}(r_{n-3} - q_{n-2} \cdot r_{n-2})$$

$$= (-q_{n-1}) \cdot r_{n-3} + [1 + q_{n-2}q_{n-1}] \cdot r_{n-2}$$

$$= [1 + q_{n-2}q_{n-1}](r_{n-4} - q_{n-3} \cdot r_{n-3}) - q_{n-1} \cdot r_{n-3}$$

$$= [\ldots] \cdot r_{n-4} + [\ldots] \cdot r_{n-3}$$

$$\vdots$$

$$= x \cdot r_0 + y \cdot r_1 = x \cdot a + y \cdot b.$$

The expressions get uglier and uglier, but even the wildest expression in parentheses is a harmless integer (which is a little consolation). Convince yourself by solving Exercises 5 and 6 that this procedure is not nearly as terrifying as it may seem.

We note the most important fact of this section (for our purposes).

Suppose that a and b are integers that are relatively prime (that is, their gcd is 1). Then there is an integer c satisfying

$$b \cdot c \bmod a = 1.$$

This may be restated as: *c is the inverse of b modulo a.*

This fact follows quickly from the previous result. With that notation we have $d = r_n = 1$. Hence there are integers x and y such that

$$1 = d = a \cdot x + b \cdot y.$$

Since $a \cdot x$ is a multiple of a, $b \cdot y$ necessarily has remainder 1 if divided by a. In other words,

$$b \cdot y \bmod a = 1.$$

The assertion follows with $c := y$.

The preceding considerations have been long and, perhaps, somewhat tedious. It would therefore be wise to summarize the important points.

- The Euclidean algorithm may be performed extremely efficiently by a computer.

In particular we note the following.

- It is very easy to compute the gcd of two integers and, in particular, to decide whether they are relatively prime.

- If a and b are relatively prime, then one can very easily compute an integer c satisfying

$$b \cdot c \bmod a = 1.$$

Key Generation.   Before we describe how the RSA algorithm works, we must clarify the hypotheses for the system. First, every participant must get a pair of keys. A key center chooses two distinct large primes p and q and multiplies them:

$$n = pq.$$

Then the center computes

$$\phi(n) = \phi(pq) = (p - 1)(q - 1).$$

(see previous section). Finally, the center computes two integers d and e with

$$e \cdot d \bmod \phi(n) = 1.$$

The participant gets e and n as his public key and d as his private key.

Remarks:

- No participant P needs to know his secret parameters p, q, and $\phi(n)$. This ignorance might even be advisable, since it is crucial that the other participants not know these numbers. Otherwise they could without any difficulty compute P's private key.

For this reason we do not recommend this key generation as a task for the individual user, though there are secure procedures for achieving this goal.

If the keys are generated centrally it is advisable to delete the data used for the computation of the keys immediately after delivery of the key.

- One of the numbers e or d, usually e, may be chosen with the goal of convenience in mind. This means that the center can choose e in such a way that it becomes easy to compute $m^e \bmod n$. For instance, it has been proposed to choose the fourth Fermat number $F_4 = 2^{2^4} + 1 = 65,537$ for the public exponent e. Since the binary representation of this number is simply 1 0000 0000 0000 0001 it is relatively easy to multiply exponentially with this number (see exercise 10.). Of course, the participants would have to have different n's; but that would be enough to guarantee that their secret keys are different.

- What are the problems with key generation? Let us first ask the question: Where do we *not* find problems? There is no problem in computing d and e: the key center first picks an e, either as described in the previous remark, or perhaps by taking any prime not dividing $\phi(n)$. Another approach would be to choose a random e, compute the gcd of e and $\phi(n)$ using the Euclidean algorithm, and then divide e by this gcd. Then one would compute a corresponding d using, perhaps, the Euclidean algorithm (see section 5.3.2). Of course, computing $\phi(n)$ is no problem—if one knows p and q.

Finding prime numbers is, of course, a common mathematical pursuit. Surely you have now and then read in the newspapers of a new world record for primes. The clear implication that such feats are formidable might well shake one's confidence in the RSA algorithm, since any user needs two primes. In other words, one needs prime numbers in abundance. If you also take into account that primes used for the RSA algorithm have a suggested length of about 100 to 200 decimal digits, you might start to worry about where these primes will be found. In fact, it is not so difficult; one does not necessarily need proper prime numbers, but pseudoprimes. These are readily available integers satisfying all (or most) of the known criteria for primes. We won't elaborate on them here, but refer the reader to the literature (see, for instance, [Gor85] and [Mau90]).

Using the RSA algorithm. If somebody wants to send a message to Mrs. Rivate, he first must learn Rivate's public key. This public key consists of the modulus n and the exponent e.

Next, the message must have the form of one or more positive integers $m \leq n$. There are many ways to achieve this; one method follows. Suppose that the message consists of letters, numbers and special characters (full stop, colon, space, etc.). Each character is represented by its own arrangement of eight bits (zeros and ones); most computers use a standard system called ASCII (an acronym, pronounced "ass-key," which stands for American Standard Code for Information Interchange; see, for instance, [BP82]). In Table 5.1, we have listed some ASCII characters.

As an example, the sequence of characters

NO WAY!

translates into

01001110 01001111 00100000 01010111 01000001 01011001 00100001

So, if n has 512 bits (which is a typical figure), one forms groups of 64 characters each, encodes these characters and gets strings of $64 \cdot 8 = 512$ bits. These bit strings are then interpreted as the binary representations of some numbers m.

We don't need to be concerned with the encoding procedure. We shall simply assume that our message is a positive integer $m \leq n$. One enciphers such a number m raising it to the eth power and reducing the result modulo n. In other words, if

$$c := m^e \bmod n,$$

then c is the ciphertext corresponding to the cleartext m.

How does one decipher c? This has been arranged in such a way that only one person can do it, namely the recipient Mrs. Rivate. She simply applies her private key to the cipher text c. More precisely, the number

$$m' := c^d \bmod n$$

is the message Mrs. Rivate gets by deciphering c. This leaves one obvious question. Mrs. Rivate does not care about an arbitrary message m'; she wants to get the original message m. Is $m' = m$? The following theorem asserts that this is always the case (provided that the enciphering and deciphering procedures were carried out correctly).

ASCII character	binary representation	ASCII character	binary representation
(space)	00100000	H	01001000
!	00100001	I	01001001
0	00110000	J	01001010
1	00110001	K	01001011
2	00110010	L	01001100
3	00110011	M	01001101
4	00110100	N	01001110
5	00110101	O	01001111
6	00110110	P	01010000
7	00110111	Q	01010001
8	00111000	R	01010010
9	00111001	S	01010011
A	01000001	T	01010100
B	01000010	U	01010101
C	01000011	V	01010110
D	01000100	W	01010111
E	01000101	X	01011000
F	01000110	Y	01011001
G	01000111	Z	01011010

TABLE 5.1
Some ASCII characters

Theorem. *For any positive integer $m \leq n$ we have $m' = m$. In other words, the above deciphering algorithm works correctly.*

The proof proceeds in several steps. In order to get some practice, we state first a condition that is easy to prove.

Step 0.

$$m' = c^d \bmod n = m^{e \cdot d} \bmod n.$$

In other words, the deciphering algorithm works correctly if and only if

$$m^{e \cdot d} \bmod n = m \text{ for all positive integers } m.$$

Step p. We have

$$m^{e \cdot d} \bmod p = m \text{ for all positive integers } m.$$

In order to demonstrate this, we first point out that d and e have been chosen in such a way that

$$e \cdot d \bmod \phi(n) = 1.$$

Therefore, there exists a nonnegative integer k such that

$$e \cdot d = 1 + k \cdot \phi(n) = 1 + k \cdot (p - 1)(q - 1),$$

since $\phi(n) = \phi(p \cdot q) = (p - 1) \cdot (q - 1)$.

Now we apply Euler's Theorem in its simplest form (alias Fermat's Little Theorem), namely, the case in which $n = p$. In order to do this we would like for m and p to be relatively prime. Of course, this is in general not going to be the case, since the assertion should be valid for all integers m. What happens if m and p are not relatively prime? Then, necessarily, p divides m since p is a prime number. In other words,

$$m \bmod p = 0.$$

Since p divides m, p divides m^{ed}. Thus we have also

$$m^{e \cdot d} \bmod p = 0.$$

The two congruences yield together

$$m^{e \cdot d} \bmod p = m.$$

Hence our assertion is true for this special case. We may therefore suppose (w.l.o.g.—"without loss of generality"—as a mathematician would wisely remark) that m and p are relatively prime.

Euler's Theorem states that

$$m^{\phi(p)} \bmod p = 1.$$

Since $\phi(p) = p - 1$, we successively get

$$m^{e \cdot d} \bmod p = m^{1 + k\phi(n)} \bmod p = m \cdot m^{k \cdot \phi(n)} \bmod p$$
$$= m \cdot m^{k \cdot (q-1)(p-1)} \bmod p = m(m^{p-1})^{k(q-1)} \bmod p$$
$$= m \cdot 1^{k \cdot (q-1)} \bmod p$$
$$= m \cdot 1 = m.$$

Hence the assertion of Step p is true for all integers m.

It is obvious what the next step will be. We skip its proof.

Step q. For every positive integer m we have

$$m^{e \cdot d} \bmod q = m.$$

It is now easy to combine the two steps and complete the proof.

Step n. For any positive integer m, we have

$$m^{e \cdot d} \bmod n = m, \text{ therefore } m' = m.$$

We demonstrate this as follows. By steps p and q we know that

$$p \text{ divides } m^{e \cdot d} - m \text{ and } q \text{ divides } m^{e \cdot d} - m.$$

So, the two primes p and q divide the same number $z := m^{e \cdot d} - m$. Since p and q are *distinct* primes, it follows that also their product $p \cdot q$ is a divisor of z. Translating this back we get the assertion

$$m^{e \cdot d} \bmod p \cdot q = m, \text{ or } m^{e \cdot d} \bmod n = m.$$

This is the claim of Step n. Therefore the theorem is proved.

The Strength of the RSA Algorithm. In the preceding section we have seen that the recipient of a message may decipher it correctly. But why should he be the only person who is able to do so? The answer seems to be simple. In order to decipher something one needs the private key d—this key being exclusively in the hands of the recipient.

We repeat, the answer *seems* to be simple, for one must ask two questions. *Can one deduce the private key from the public key?* For the deciphering algorithm described above, clearly one needs the private key. But it is conceivable that there exist *fundamentally different deciphering algorithms.* So the second question is: *Is it possible to decipher the message without using the private key?* We shall discuss both questions, but, admittedly, without reaching a final conclusion.

Suppose that we know the public key—that is, the numbers e and n. How could we compute from this the private key d? Naturally, if we knew $\phi(n)$, then we could compute d; we could proceed as the key generation center and compute d using the Euclidean algorithm, for instance.

So far, so good. We have reduced the problem to the computation of $\phi(n)$. How can we find $\phi(n)$? If we knew the decomposition of n into its primes p and q, then we trivially could compute $\phi(n) = (p - 1)(q - 1)$. Interestingly enough, the converse is also true. If we knew n and $\phi(n)$, then we could factor n. (Indeed, in this situation we have the two equations

$$p \cdot q = n \text{ and } (p - 1)(q - 1) = \phi(n)$$

for the two unknowns p and q. So, we could solve for p and q.) To sum up, if n is the product of two distinct primes, then computing $\phi(n)$ is the same as factoring n (see exercise 16).

So, everything would be very easy *if* we could factor n—and there's the rub. Of course, to the casual eye the obstacle is not immediately obvious; it is a popular belief that since there is no difficulty in factoring integers like 72, 123, or 221, it necessarily follows that factoring larger integers remains relatively easy. But the factorization of even rather small integers like 1763 or 8633 (each a product of two primes) imposes considerable difficulties for a human brain. Considering that the n appearing in the RSA algorithm has a suggested length of about 200 decimal digits, one gets a strong feeling that factoring such large integers is an extremely difficult problem.

Now I must confess, to my eternal shame, that mathematics itself (which is, after all, the mother that gave birth to such problems) cannot do much more than utter this feeling—though in a very precise way.

What can mathematics say with certainty? How can one decompose a large integer n into its prime factors? A naive approach is to proceed systematically. In other words, one tries every integer $m \leq n$ to see whether or not it is a divisor of n. Of course, it is not necessary to test all integers $\leq n$. We may restrict ourselves to primes between 2 and $\sqrt{n}$. (For, if $n = p \cdot q$, then $p \leq \sqrt{n}$ or $q \leq \sqrt{n}$.) This is a safe procedure, but a very, very lengthy one. For instance, in order to test a 200-digit number, in the worst case, one has to consider all primes between 2 and 10^{100}.

Naturally, mathematicians have not been lazy and have invented many sophisticated algorithms. But for our problem (namely, factoring a product of two equally large primes) these algorithms are almost useless.

An example may illustrate this. In 1990 the ninth Fermat number $F_9 = 2^{2^9} + 1 = 2^{512} + 1$, a notorious number on the world's most-wanted list, was factored. This 513-bit number (having more than 155 decimal digits) was shown to be the product of three primes having 7, 49, and 99 decimal digits. Although some clever new mathematical algorithms were devised for the task, the crucial element for success was the ability to break the problem into small parts so that the work could be "decentralized." Collaborators all over the world did their small share and sent in their results (see [LM90]). The partial solutions were put together, and Arjen K. Lenstra and Mark S. Manasse completed the factorization.

This success was sufficiently exciting to be reported in newspapers around the world; naturally it added fuel to the heated discussion about the security of the RSA algorithm and its relatives. Supporters of the RSA were fast to point out that F_9 is certainly not a number that would have been chosen as the modulus in the RSA algorithm. Let us summarize some of the relevant points of the ensuing discussion.

- No one has yet found a good factoring algorithm. Some people are therefore inclined to believe that there is none. Furthermore, the "number field sieve" that was used by Lenstra and Manasse is effective only for numbers of the form $a^b + c$, with small a and c. It seems that factoring a randomly chosen number with 120 decimal digits is still an extremely difficult problem by today's standards.

- Can someone at least prove that a good factoring algorithm cannot exist? No, even this has not been possible. It seems that the factoring problem is so difficult that we cannot even prove that it is difficult.

- The answer to the question of how many bits a number must have to resist a factoring attack is still a matter of faith. Proponents of the RSA algorithms stress the fact that no 512-bit RSA number has yet been factored, so there should be no problem in using moduli of approximately 512 bits. On the other hand, factoring enthusiasts point to the enormous progress in the development of factoring algorithms and warn: If you really need a secure RSA, then don't settle for less than 1024 bits.

To sum up: One way to defeat the RSA algorithm is to factor n; at present no other attack on the algorithm is known. The problem of decomposing integers into their prime factors belongs among the most difficult and famous problems of mathematics. But then, to base the security of a cryptosystem on the fact that at present no mathematician has been able to invent a good algorithm to break it is a grievous insult to mathematics.

One final question: There are abundant papers, talks, books, lectures, and so forth on the RSA algorithm, yet it is seldom used—why? The reason is simple. Only very recently have good implementations been designed. There are now software versions being used for electronic signatures that take approximately one second for a signature of a 512-bit modulus. (These are slow, but show promise.) Also, single-chip hardware has been developed on which the RSA algorithm runs at a speed of 10 kbits/s. (There are even specially designed RSA boards available achieving a speed of 100 kbits/s.) Taking into account that the future ISDN network will allow 64 kbits/s and that today's local area networks can convey 10 Mbits/s (that is, 10,000 kbits/s = 10,000,000 bits per second), it becomes clear that the first commercial applications of the RSA algorithm will be electronic signature and key exchange.

5.4 KEY EXCHANGE

In view of the fact that today's implementations of public key algorithms are rather slow (while there are good and very fast implementations of symmetric algorithms available), it makes sense to try to combine the two types of algorithms, exploiting each system's advantages. The fundamental idea of a *hybrid system* is as follows.

Essentially, one uses a symmetric algorithm. A public key encryption system is used only for the exchange of the secret keys necessary for the symmetric algorithm. Here the bad performance of the public key algorithm is not a bottleneck for the whole system; the keys to be exchanged are tiny messages (with typical sizes of 56 or 128 bits) and the actual exchange is relatively infrequent. (A key change for every session is not very often necessary, though occasionally it would be desirable.)

Such a secure key exchange is performed using a public key encryption scheme. In order to send a secret key k to Mr. Blic, one must encipher k using Mr. Blic's public key. Then Mr. Blic deciphers the received value c with his private key and obtains k (see Figure 5.6).

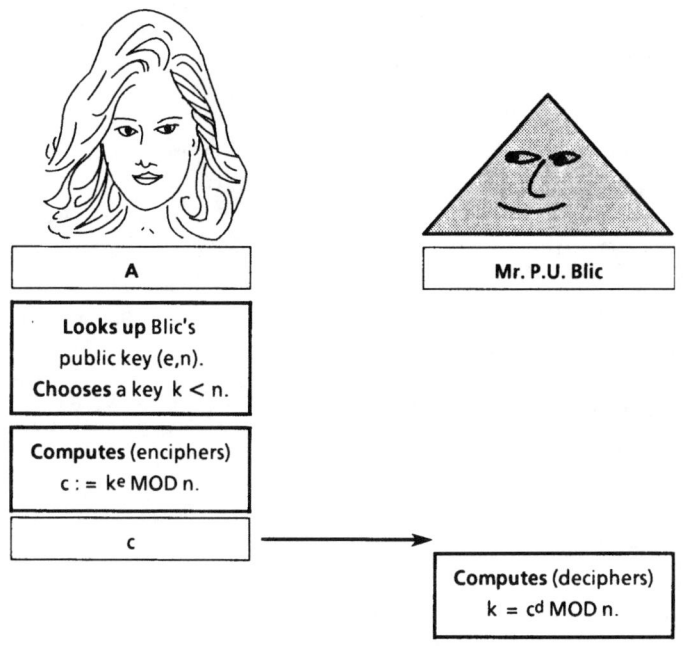

FIGURE 5.6
RSA key exchange

This procedure works perfectly; it has only one (more or less philosophical) disadvantage. It is A who sends B a key, in order that A and B can communicate. From an abstract point of view one might say that both parties should *agree* upon a key, rather than one of them choosing a key and sending it to the other. Using such a key generation both parties would play exactly the same role.

As a matter of fact there is such a system; it is very practical, and, remarkably enough, this system was proposed in the very first paper on public key cryptography, the famous "New Directions" paper by Diffie and Hellman [DH76]. Diffie [Dif88] writes

Marty and I continued twisting exponentials around in our minds and discussions trying to make them fit. Marty eventually made the breakthrough early one morning in May 1976 .... Marty called and explained exponential key exchange in its unnerving simplicity. Listening to him, I

realized that the notion had been at the edge of my mind for some time, but had never really broken through.

This "exponential key exchange scheme" is nowadays called the *Diffie–Hellman key exchange scheme*. I will describe this system first in mathematical terms, and then bring the description down to earth.

Two participants who wish to agree upon a secret key must have already agreed upon two things, a prime p and a positive integer $s < p$, both of which may be public. So, for instance, all participants could use the same p and s. It is recommended that s is one of the $\phi(p - 1)$ numbers that are relatively prime to $p - 1$.

The scheme is simple. A and B choose integers $a, b < p$, respectively. A computes

$$\alpha = s^a \bmod p,$$

and B computes

$$\beta = s^b \bmod p.$$

Each sends the result of his calculations to the other. Then A forms

$$k = \beta^a \bmod p$$

and B computes

$$\alpha^b \bmod p.$$

Since

$$\alpha^b \bmod p = (s^a)^b \bmod p = s^{ab} \bmod p$$

and

$$\beta^a \bmod p = (s^b)^a \bmod p = s^{ba} \bmod p = s^{ab} \bmod p,$$

both get the same values $k = s^{ab} \bmod p$.

Figure 5.7 illustrates how both sides have equal rights.

Either they take this number directly as their common key, or perform an agreed-upon modification in order to obtain the key required by the

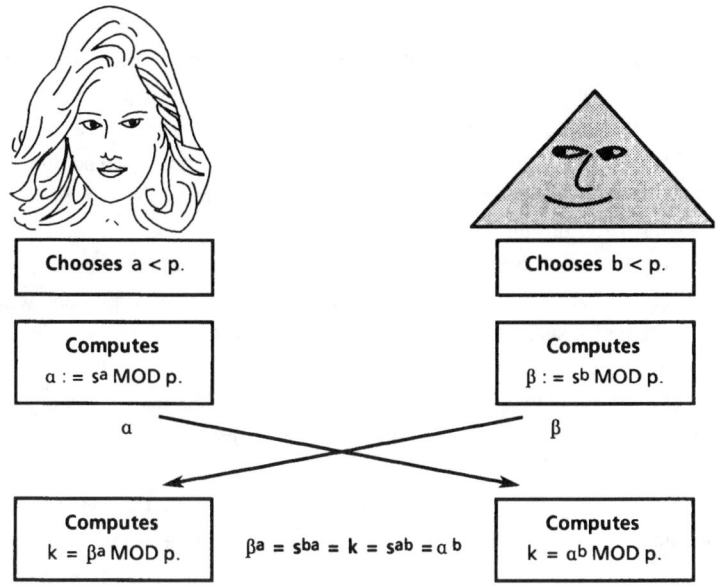

FIGURE 5.7
Diffie–Hellman key exchange

symmetric algorithm. For instance, they could take the first 56 bits of the binary representation of k.

Why is this scheme secure against an attack of Mr. X from outside? He knows α and β. If he could deduce a from α or b from β then he could compute k just as A or B did. But, as a matter of fact, *it is not feasible to deduce a, knowing* $\alpha = s^a$. The problem of computing a, given $s^a \bmod p$, is known as taking the *discrete logarithm*.

An example might illustrate how difficult the problem is. Suppose $p = 11$ and $s = 4$. If we play the role of A, it is easy to compute

$$s^4 = 4^4 = 4^2 \cdot 4^2 = 5 \cdot 5 \bmod 11 = 3 \bmod 11.$$

But, if Mr. X knows only that $s^a = 4^a = 3 \bmod 11$, it is much more difficult to see what a is. The reader should solve this relatively easy exercise and also try to solve Exercise 17.

There is one observation that might well favor Mr. X's position. It is not absolutely clear that he must uncover one of the numbers a or b. Mr. X (to whom we attribute extraordinary intelligence) might discover some clever way of computing the secret information k directly from α and β. However, there is bad news for Mr. X: no one yet has found a means to do so. On the other hand, no one can show that breaking the Diffie–Hellman scheme is equivalent to computing the discrete logarithm.

Note that using the Diffie-Hellman key exchange one can answer the following "paradoxical" question in the affirmative: Can two persons who have never had a secret in common, by a public discussion agree upon a common secret?

Our key exchange scheme can also be accomplished over any alphabet with p^m elements, where p is a prime. If $m > 1$, one uses not the integers modulo p^m, but the finite field with p^m elements, denoted by GF(p^m) (the Galois field, named after the brilliant but tragically unlucky Evariste Galois, 1811–1832). Very recently, problems concerning discrete logarithms have extended far beyond the scope of this book; the interested reader may consult [Kob87].

I shall present a visualization of the Diffie–Hellman key exchange (Figure 5.8).

The program runs as follows. Both parties get identical copies of a suitcase (which contains the common key k) locked with two locks, one that can be opened by A, and one that can be opened by B. First, both release their respective locks on the suitcases they have got and send the suitcase to the other party. Having received the suitcases, A and B may release the remaining locks. It is only then that the suitcases may be opened to betray their secret keys. Now A and B may communicate secretly using the secret key k.

5.5 OTHER USES OF THE DISCRETE LOGARITHM

Interestingly, the difficulty of taking discrete logarithms is applicable not only to key management, but also to the design of enciphering and signature algorithms. There are presently two such protocols known; one is the work of Taher ElGamal of Hewlett-Packard in Palo Alto [ElG85], and the other was developed by Jim Massey of ETH Zurich and Jim Omura (who was

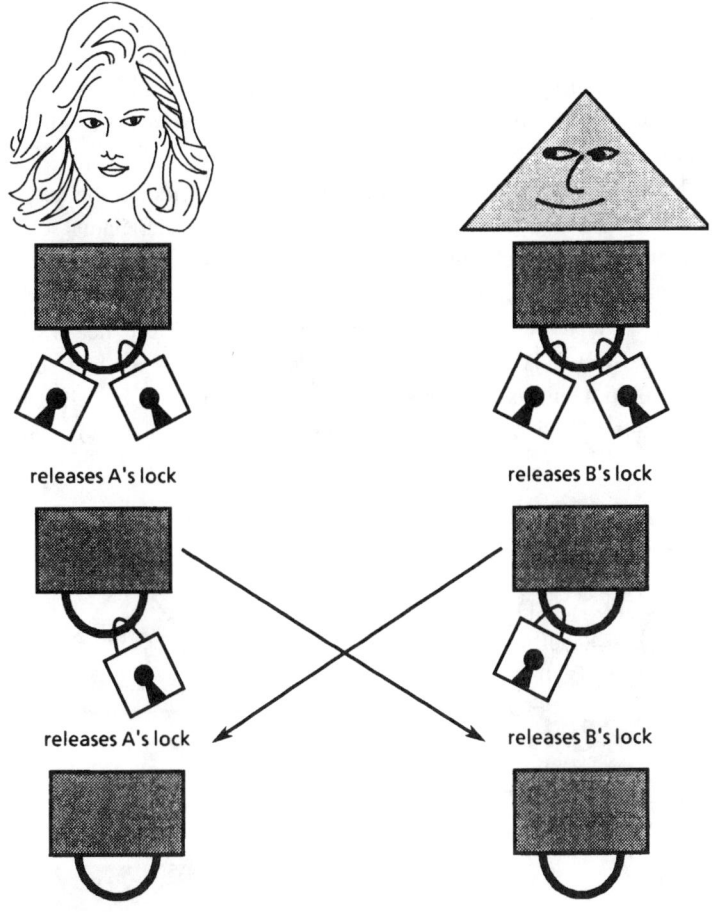

FIGURE 5.8
The Diffie–Hellman key exchange (using suitcases)

then at the University of California). The ElGamal scheme can be seen as a variant of the Diffie–Hellman scheme with an enciphering algorithm incorporated. We shall first briefly discuss this protocol and then present the Massey–Omura scheme because it is so neat.

In the ElGamal scheme there is a general agreement upon a prime p and an integer s. Participant B has as his secret key an integer b^* and as his public key the number $\beta = s^{b^*} \bmod p$. If A wants to send B an enciphered message

m, she chooses an integer a and then computes two numbers, $s^a \bmod p$ and, using B's public key, the number $k = (\beta)^a \bmod p$, which will be used as the key for enciphering the message m. A applies any symmetric algorithm f to m obtaining the ciphertext $c = f_k(m)$. Finally, she sends B two pieces of data, the number $s^a \bmod p$ as well as the ciphertext c.

Using his secret key b^*, B can compute from $s^a \bmod p$ the key $k = (s^a)^{b^*} \bmod p$, and then decipher c. (Note that in the original ElGamal scheme, the algorithm f was just multiplication $\bmod p$, that is, $c = k \cdot m \bmod p$; but this is an unnecessary limitation.)

Let's now turn to the *Massey–Omura scheme*. The basic idea is simple (see Figure 5.9). If A wants to encipher a message for B, she first puts the message into a suitcase, secures it by her lock, and sends it to B. He, of course, cannot open A's lock, but he can secure the message also using his

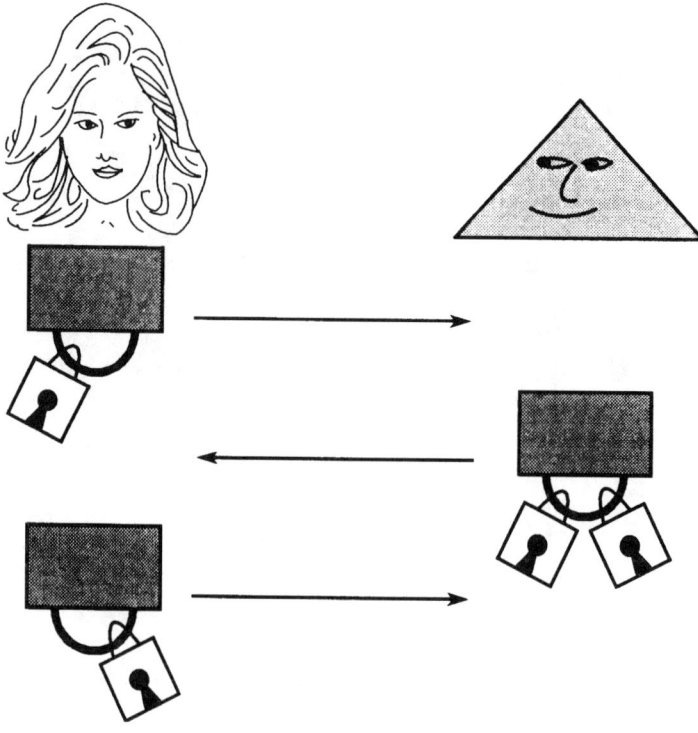

FIGURE 5.9
Shamir's no-key algorithm

lock. Then this doubly locked message is sent back to A. Now she may unlock her lock (being no longer able to read the message) and send it again to B. Finally, he removes his lock and can read the message. This procedure is also called Shamir's no-key algorithm.

Can one realize such an idea for transmission of electronic data? The answer is yes—using discrete logarithms. This method was presented at the first EUROCRYPT conference in Udine, Italy. Let us suppose that all participants have agreed upon a public prime p. Now, each user U chooses two positive integers e_U and d_U such that

$$e_U \cdot d_U \bmod p - 1 = 1.$$

We have described on page 109 how to compute d_U from e_U. We know also that, by Euler's Theorem,

$$m^{e_U d_U} \bmod p = m$$

for all integers $m < p$.

In contrast with the RSA algorithm, the users keep *both* of these numbers secret, publishing neither of them. (In fact, if Mr. X knows e_U he is able to compute d_U, since the modulus p is public knowledge.) Now, consider the situation in which a message m is sent in cipher from A to our participant B. We may assume that m is represented by a number (or a sequence of numbers) less than p.

First A computes $m^{e_A} \bmod p$ and sends this to B; B in turn computes the e_Bth power of the number he has received and returns the result $m^{e_A e_B} \bmod p$ to A. Now A applies her number d_A to what she has received and gets $m^{e_A e_B d_A} \bmod p$, which turns out to be

$$m^{e_A e_B d_A} \bmod p = m^{e_A d_A e_B} \bmod p = m^{e_B} \bmod p,$$

by the properties of e_A and d_A. The result is sent to B who applies d_B to it and obtains

$$m^{e_B d_B} \bmod p = m$$

(see Figure 5.10).

In what sense does this protocol rely on the difficulty of taking discrete logarithms? How could Mr. X get hold of B's secrets e_B and d_B? Easily

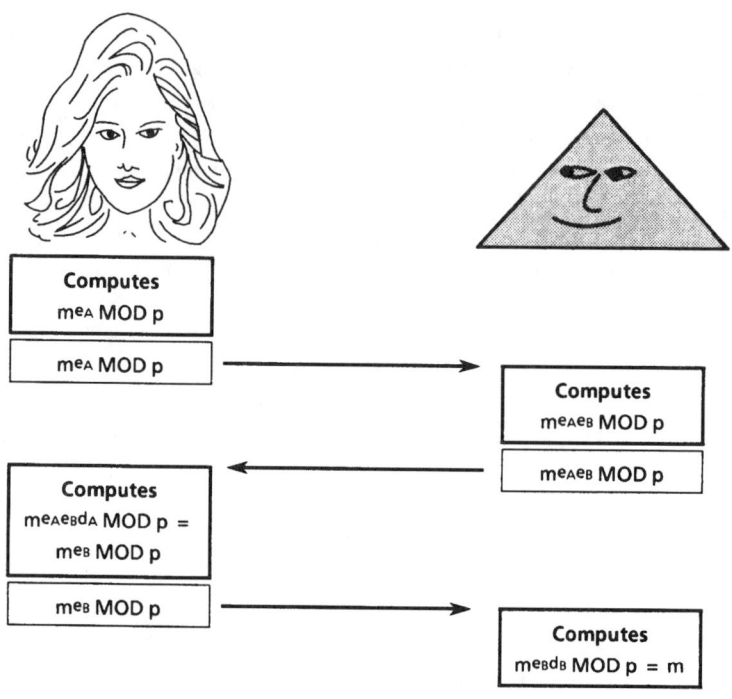

FIGURE 5.10
The Massey–Omura protocol

enough—if only he could compute discrete logarithms. All he would have to do is to send B a number m. If B follows the protocol, he sends back

$$m^+ = m^{e_B} \bmod p.$$

Clearly, if Mr. X could compute the discrete logarithm of m^+, he would obtain e_B and then proceed (by applying Euclid's algorithm) to obtain d_B.

There are two other public key encryption schemes, namely, the McEliece scheme [McE78] based on error correcting codes, and the Knapsack algorithm proposed by Merkle and Hellman [MH78]. The latter algorithm is of questionable value now, having effectively been broken by Shamir [Sha82].

A final remark is in order. Both the public key exchange and the Diffie–Hellman key exchange work perfectly in the sense that one does not need a secret channel for sending the keys. But one nevertheless needs *trust*. By this I mean that we work under the hypothesis that neither of the participants is cheating. In the Diffie–Hellman scheme, B has to trust that the α he receives is indeed a power of s. In our suitcase example (Figure 5.8), both parties have to trust that the secrets in both "identical" suitcases are in fact identical.

In the language of chapter 4, the key exchange schemes described above do not require a secret channel but an authentic channel. (And some experts seriously ask whether in practice we have gained very much.)

EXERCISES

1. Exercise your imagination. Interpret the following scenario (Figure 5.11) as a public-key encryption scheme. Each participant provides a suitcase with a name sticker attached. The opened suitcases are open to the public. Each may be closed just by pressing its two halves together, but in order to reopen it a person needs a key—the unique key that fits it.

   Explain the idea of public key cryptography using this example.

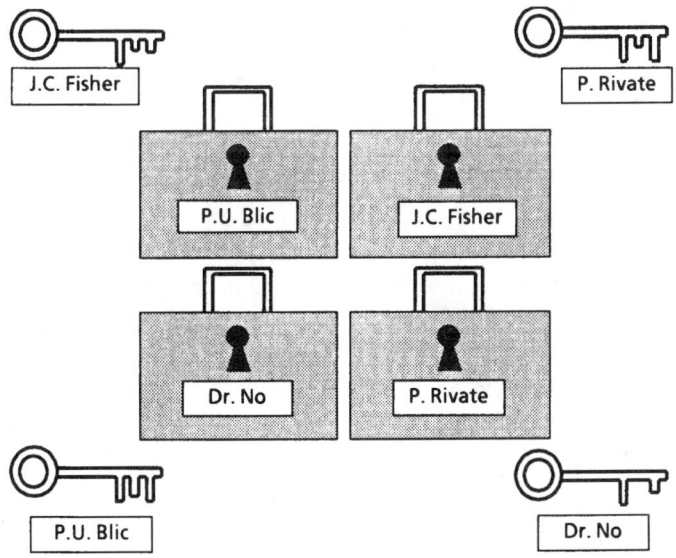

FIGURE 5.11
The suitcase example

2. Apply a transposition cipher to Peter A. Schlaube in order to obtain a name that you certainly have read.

3. Show that the Euclidean algorithm does in fact yield the greatest common divisor of two integers a and b.

@ 4. Write a program for the Euclidean algorithm.

5. Compute integers x and y with the property that

$$3 = 792x + 75y.$$

6. (a) Compute integers x and y with the property that

$$1 = 17x + 55y.$$

(b) Compute $(2/17) \bmod 55$ and $(2/55) \bmod 17$. (Hint: Multiply your outcome in part (a) by 2 and note that $17 = 55y \bmod 55 = 0$.)

@ 7. Write a program that has as its input two positive integers a and b and as its output integers x and y satisfying

$$\gcd(a, b) = a \cdot x + b \cdot y.$$

8. What is the gcd of 2166 and 6099?

9. For $p = 23$ and $q = 37$, compute integers d and e according to the RSA algorithm and encipher the message $m = 537$.

10. (a) How many multiplications do you need in order to compute m^{16}? (Hint: Observe that $m^{16} = (((m^2)^2)^2)^2$.)

(b) How many multiplications do you need in order to compute m^{21}?

▷ (c) Can you formulate a "fast" algorithm for computing m^d? (Hint: Use the binary representation of d. This algorithm is called the *square-and-multiply algorithm*.)

▷ (d) Roughly how many multiplications does one need in order to compute m^d?

11. Convince yourself that the theorem of Euler was used only in the simplest case where $n = p$ is a prime.

The next three exercises outline a proof of Euler's theorem in the case $n = p$. (See [Hon73], pp. 1–3 for details.)

12. Let p be a prime. Show that the binomial coefficient

$$\binom{p}{i} = \frac{p \cdot (p-1) \cdot \cdots \cdot 2 \cdot 1}{i \cdot (i-1) \cdot \cdots \cdot 2 \cdot 1 \cdot (p-i) \cdot (p-i-1) \cdot \cdots \cdot 2 \cdot 1}$$

is an integer that is divisible by p, if $1 < i < p$.

13. Let p be a prime. Then for any two integers a and b, show that

$$(a + b)^p \bmod p = a^p + b^p \bmod p.$$

(Hint: Use the binomial theorem.)

14. Let p be a prime. Then for any positive integer m, show that

$$m^p \bmod p = m.$$

(Hint: Use mathematical induction on m.)

▷ 15. In order to prevent a person from abusing a public key system by introducing his own unauthorized public keys, one proceeds as follows. Any valid public key E is certified by a hopefully trustworthy Certification Authority CA. To do this, CA forms the signature of E using the center's private key. Before a participant uses the public key E of another participant, the signature will be verified by using the public key of the center CA.

Convince yourself that the misuse described at the end of section 5.1 is rendered impossible by this procedure. The problem has now been reduced to controlling a relatively small number of certification authorities. The solution sketched above is part of a general method which is explained in a standard called X.509 [CCITT].

16. If I tell you that
    (a) the integer 14,803 is the product of just two primes, and
    (b) $\phi(14,803) = 14,560$,
    can you now factor 14,803?

@ 17. Write a program that factors integers having eight or fewer digits. See how long it takes your program to factor 12,863,273 ($= 3259 \cdot 3947$), and 1,111,111 ($= 239 \cdot 4649$).

18. Assume you know that $7^a \bmod 31 = 10$. What is a?

19. Write down the ElGamal encryption scheme using an "arrow diagram."

20. Explain carefully the difference between the Diffie–Hellman key exchange scheme and the ElGamal scheme. Is the difference of a cryptographic nature?

21. Does the Massey–Omura algorithm have disadvantages? What are they?

Chapter 6

NO ONE KNOWS, WITH GLEE I CLAIM, THAT RUMPELSTILTSKIN IS MY NAME

or

HOW CAN WE STAY ANONYMOUS?

6.1 WHAT ANONYMITY IS ABOUT

Cryptography, by definition, is concerned with concealing messages: enciphering conceals the content of a message. But it might also be desirable to conceal the sender, or the recipient, or even the very fact that a message has been sent. Anonymity refers to any of these three senses:

- anonymity of the *sender*,
- anonymity of the *recipient*,
- anonymity of the whole *communication process*.

In this chapter I shall deal with ways to achieve anonymity.

Perhaps the reader will object: "Isn't anonymity pure luxury? Even though it might be theoretically attainable, whenever there is considerable cost involved anyone—at least any honest person—can live without it!" Well, such a point of view certainly has merit. This calls for a moment of thought.

Balancing the needs of the community against the needs of the individual is a fundamental problem of democracy. Each gain for the rights of an individual is paid for in lost rights on behalf of society at large, and vice versa. An increase in an individual's right to privacy, for example, costs society an equal measure of control.

The ever-increasing role of the computer in our lives throws this delicate balance out of equilibrium, giving both big business and government access to information about individuals, and opening the way to abuses of power that go well beyond the nightmarish scenario of Orwell's *1984*. The private citizen today has little control over how such information is used; indeed, there is no way of knowing whether information that is routinely exchanged by organizations, both public and private, is inaccurate, obsolete, or just plain malicious.

But equally frightening is the potential for abuse by individuals: fraud of all kinds, involving checks, consumer credit, and social services, is easier than ever before. The cure for such abuses *against* society is, of course, more efficient, pervasive, and impregnable computerized record-keeping systems. And so it goes. Maybe there is no simple answer. Let's look at some specific considerations.

1. There are situations in which everyone agrees that anonymity is necessary. Certainly elections should be secret. Consider electronic voting: while the result of the election must be accurate, the voters (that is, the senders of the votes) must remain anonymous.

   Another example regards scientific research based on sensitive personal data—medical data concerning drug abuse or involving the disease AIDS comes quickly to mind. Here it is crucial that scientists have all relevant data without anyone being able to infer the identity of the person the data come from. In other words, what one needs is sender anonymity.

   There are many niches in any society which require relative anonymity. Think, for instance, of Alcoholics Anonymous. Here anonymity is, in the opinion of the people supporting this institution, essential for the recuperation process.

2. In everyday life we have a perfect example of sender anonymity, namely money, particularly coins. Pardon? Well, a coin does not carry its history with it. If I have a coin in my hand perhaps I know the person I got it from, but I have no information whatsoever of who has used this coin and for what purpose.

   This system works so well that it serves as a model for most of the concepts dealing with sender anonymity. We shall look at one such concept in section 6.3. But note that at least part of the evil associated with money can be attributed to its anonymity: it is an ideal medium for crime. Some people will do anything for money; they are anonymous when acquiring their filthy lucre, but rich, powerful, respected—and untraceable!—when spending it.

3. With new electronic media there even seems to be a market for anonymity in electronic networks. For instance, in the extremely popular videotex system *Teletel* in France there is a channel called "Kiosque" in which the users can speak to one another anonymously. Of course, this is a low level of sender anonymity since all users are known to the operating company—they are, after all, billed for the service. The users are anonymous only to one another, and this is guaranteed by the operating company. Interestingly, although this service is rather expensive, it is quite popular. Perhaps part of the attraction is a lively repartee that does not always adhere, to say the least, to the rules of middle-class respectability. But here again there is a dark side. People will say things they wouldn't dare say if anyone knew who was saying it. This is closely related to "mob mentality," where people do things as part of a mob—that is, anonymously—that they wouldn't even consider doing otherwise.

4. One important application of anonymity within the field of cryptology is key generation. In all countries that use cryptology, there is probably a security center in charge of generating the keys that are later used to encipher diplomatic messages between the government and its various embassies. My guess is that the poor guy who actually handles the keys is not very well paid. So, if he knew that a certain key would be used next month to encipher the traffic between, say, Washington and Bogota, there would be a real danger—either to the message or to the messenger, or to both. What is required is anonymity. But one needs more: one must be able to prove that the key generation is performed with anonymity. (Imagine a situation in which the poor guy doesn't know anything, but some enemy does not believe him.)

5. All aspects of anonymity, like other cultural or political entities, change with time. Let me give you an example of a process which certainly belongs today to one's very private life, but in earlier times was considered quite differently. Just 200 years ago the call of nature was, at least in Europe, answered in public. There was a professional known as a "Notdurftanbieter," a sort of medieval emergency road service, whose duty was to wrap the client in a coat, preserving very little anonymity in the

process. (The reader who is interested in further details should consult [MBeu86].) Before dismissing this as just another example of the author's questionable taste, note that here too we see the two sides to the question of an individual's right to privacy. A cubicle in today's public washrooms is also a haven where one has the privacy required for all kinds of actions against society, ranging from some petty act of vandalism to—if we are to believe the movies—the transactions of organized crime.

In my opinion, anonymity is not a value in itself; rather, one must decide for any given application whether anonymity serves to achieve the goal of the application, and whether it is worth the price. Even though anonymity cannot easily be labeled good or bad, I am convinced that one important aim of scientific studies is to show what science can and cannot do. Then, decisions can be based on scientific grounds instead of becoming merely a matter of political maneuvering.

Be that as it may, an interesting and perhaps surprising fact is that certain models of anonymity can be obtained by cryptographic means! The aim of the present chapter is to study this aspect. After these philosophical ramblings we return to science. We begin with models for all three types of anonymity; later we shall discuss two rather more elaborate models.

Even the most detached reader browsing these pages will note that in comparison with the more-or-less established techniques discussed earlier, the ideas presented in this chapter are much more speculative. But—again, this is my opinion—it is important to develop good models which show that anonymity is possible in electronic networks, if only to show that the computer is not necessarily the Big Brother that many people, sometimes with justification, fear it to be.

6.2 THREE (TOO) SIMPLE MODELS

Anonymity of the Recipient via Broadcasting. Conceptually, it is relatively easy to achieve anonymity of the recipient by sending the message to all participants, or, at least, to many of them. Broadcast media such as radio and TV are the prototypes of such anonymity. Perhaps you recall instances where authorities spoke directly via TV to kidnappers? Such a procedure guarantees perfect anonymity for the recipients of the message.

Other examples are found in the notices one can read now and again in the classified ads of the local paper, such as the following.

Anonymity of the Sender Using Pseudonyms. A sender can hide himself under a pseudonym (a name assumed to hide one's true identity). He may even use one pseudonym for each communication partner; if he is even more wary, he may use a separate pseudonym for each session. Under such circumstances the sender can completely disguise his identity; from the outside, he is as hard to find as the proverbial needle in a haystack.

The difficulties of such a procedure are obvious. The sender must not lose track of his pseudonyms. What's more, the problem of transferring confidential information from one pseudonym to another is very difficult and without a completely satisfactory solution.

Anonymity of the Communication Relationship using Dummy Messages. To prevent outsiders from observing the arrival of a particular message—"Caesar's aide-de-camp was seen talking with Cleopatra at 11.30 P.M."—one should send messages *very often*, even continuously. This means that one must send dummy messages. A Mr. X who intends to make out a communication profile of a particular participant has to record, to remember, and to analyze all messages, with the guarantee that 99.99% of the time the evaluation provides no information at all.

Two famous examples from World War II should be mentioned here.

- The U.S. knew shortly before the Japanese attacked Pearl Harbor that an attack was imminent primarily because of the increase in the number of secret messages. (Here, the absence of dummy messages provided information.)

- Long before their invasion of Normandy in 1944, the Allies began flooding the Continent with dummy messages. The German defenders apparently never knew when the real message (that the invasion was on) arrived, advising the underground to prepare the way.

The disadvantage of such a deluge of bogus messages is obvious: Although today's public networks have substantial capacity, and tomorrow's promise to be even more remarkable, their design is based on the premise that at any given time only a small percentage of all participants transmit a message. No network would survive for long should people send continuous streams of messages. Indeed, the dummy-message method would need a network capacity which is beyond the wildest dreams of even AT&T.

Now I shall present two sophisticated models which may not have any immediate application, but which can at least be discussed scientifically.

6.3 ELECTRONIC CASH

As previously mentioned, ordinary money has—among other advantages—the feature that it offers perfect anonymity to an individual: A person enters a shop, chooses some delicacy or other, pays cash, walks out—and has left no trace. Of course there is the possibility that the cashier remembers the person, but the crucial observation is that the money itself offers no hint as to who has spent it. Coins do not bear an individual history; they all are the same. What has been purchased with the coins is the business of the client and the salesman, no one else.

Imagine now an electronic cash system. Very likely, such a system would be designed to store all data for a specified time, an unavoidable necessity for the clearing process as well as a hedge against unforeseen difficulties or complaints (see the discussions in section 4.3). Such a system is the opposite of a system with anonymity. Imagine now that system being converted into an electronic cash system with customer anonymity. This seems impossible, and probably it is impossible! In order to build anonymity into an electronic cash system, one must start from scratch. But, how to start?

Amazingly enough, one can simulate coins by electronic analogues. This idea of electronic coins can be attributed to David Chaum [Cha85]—as can many profound ideas concerning electronic anonymity. He quite convincingly argues that even though his scheme was devised to protect the privacy of the individual citizen, his proposal would, at the same time, provide greater security to banks.

Generally speaking, Chaum's proposal is based on a public key cryptosystem, the RSA-algorithm in particular. Imagine that Professor Nev R. Mind would like to obtain from his bank an electronic $5 "coin." (For the sake of simplicity, we suppose that a bank can stamp coins; usually this is performed under the responsibility of the respective national bank.) Prof. Mind wants this coin to have the following properties.

- This piece of information (which is, remember, simply a string of bits!) shall be accepted by any shopkeeper (or any vending machine) as an equivalent of $5.
- Once accepted, no one has any hint that this bit string was spent by Prof. Mind.

Now, to business. For any type of coin, the bank will have a pair of keys, secret and public. So, for producing electronic $5 coins the bank has a modulus n, a public exponent e, and a secret exponent d. This is the general setting.

In order to get a $5 coin, Prof. Mind first gets down to work. He chooses two big numbers C and V at random. The number V is, in a way that will be explained, the raw material for the coin, whereas the only purpose of the random number C is to camouflage the communication between Prof. Mind and the bank.

Continuing, he forms the number W from V by writing V twice in succession. For instance, if $V = 123{,}456$, then $W = 123{,}456{,}123{,}456$. The only difficult task for Prof. Mind at this stage is to form the number

$$S := C^e \cdot W \bmod n.$$

He then sends this number S to his bank and requests the bank to turn this bitworm into a $5 coin.

Now it is the bank's turn. Of course, the first job is to debit Prof. Mind's account $5. Then the bank raises the number S to the dth power (where, remember, d is the secret $5 key), yielding

$$T := S^d \bmod n,$$

and sends T back to Prof. Mind.

Prof. Mind should verify the data he receives. He can do this by raising T to the power e; if this T correctly corresponds to his S, then

$$T^e = S^{de} = S.$$

This string T is not yet the coin, but the coin is obtained from T by dividing out the camouflage number C:

$$F := T \cdot C^{-1} \bmod n.$$

(Note that C^{-1} is the integer satisfying $C \cdot C^{-1} \bmod n = 1$. The existence of such a C^{-1} has been demonstrated on page 109.)

Now, behold, this number F is Prof. Mind's $5 coin!

But really, what is this coin? Can we compute it? Well, if there weren't any hocus-pocus about it, we'd have

$$F = T \cdot C^{-1} \bmod n = S^d \cdot C^{-1} \bmod n = C^{ed} \cdot W^d \cdot C^{-1} \bmod n$$
$$= C \cdot W^d \cdot C^{-1} \bmod n = W^d \bmod n.$$

Observe that this calculation shows that in reality F does not depend on C, but only on d and V. In fact, C serves only to cover up the tracks.

Warning: The above calculations work only from a (nonexistent) superior point of view. In reality, unless one has either Prof. Mind's knowledge of V and C or the bank's knowledge of d, one doesn't know anything about these secret numbers!

Now we must convince ourselves that the number F indeed satisfies all the claims made for it.

* *Anyone can easily verify that F is a $5-number.*

In order to check this, one raises F to the eth power (where e is the public $5-key); one obtains

$$F^e \bmod n = W^{de} \bmod n = W \bmod n.$$

For the criterion that determines whether F is a money number, one takes the property that the number $F^e \bmod n$ consists of identical right and left halves. Since exponentiation is a powerful cryptographic function (in the sense that it stirs the numbers up in an essentially random way) one cannot derive a property of F that indicates whether F^e consists of two identical halves. In other words, it is impossible to stamp coins without using the bank's secret key d.

If F is submitted to a bank, then the bank first verifies whether F is a $5 number. Then it credits $5 to the appropriate account—*but only if this particular coin has been submitted for the first time.* Such a precaution is necessary because a deceitful customer or shopkeeper might consider submitting the same $5 number F over and over; this is possible in theory, since F is simply a string of bits and no one can stop an individual of questionable intent from copying it.

- *No one can trace Prof. Mind.*

Can the shopkeeper (or anyone who has F) infer Prof. Mind's identity? The sole possibility would be to inquire at the bank of origin. But it is impossible for the bank to know to whom F was given; the bank has never seen F ($= W^d \bmod n$) before, but only the numbers

$$S = C^e \cdot W \bmod n \text{ and } T = C^{ed} \cdot W^d = C \cdot W^d \bmod n.$$

Since in both numbers known to the bank the camouflage number C occurs in an essential way, the bank is unable to correlate F with S or T. Hence *the system provides perfect customer anonymity.*

David Chaum himself illustrated the above procedure in terms of everyday objects. This simulation is not, of course, a suggestion to be taken seriously; it merely gives a vivid description of what is going on.

Professor Nev R. Mind sends a blank slip of paper to his bank. This paper is sealed inside an envelope under a piece of carbon paper. The bank does not open the envelope, but presses its $5 die onto the envelope and returns the impressed envelope to Prof. Mind. He opens the envelope, throws the carbon paper away (or even reuses it if he wants), and removes the slip of paper (which now bears the image of the $5 die); he is now able to use this paper as ready money.

As with electronic cash, the bank doesn't know who is who. Since it knows no relationship between the envelope and its contents, it cannot infer who has had the $5 coin first.

One final, important remark contrasting electronic cash with ordinary coins. With real coins the tasks of creating a new coin and of duplicating an existing coin are of equal difficulty. This is not the case with any current model of electronic coins. Here, cryptography can guarantee that no unauthorized party can create new coins. But, in contrast, it is extremely easy to duplicate a coin; one must merely copy the corresponding string of bits.

As a consequence, in all models the bank must keep a list of all the coins submitted to it. Clearly, this is an extremely expensive procedure. A new scheme [CFN90] has been proposed that has at least one feature making it more suitable as a substitute for money. If a coin is submitted only once, the customer remains in perfect anonymity, but if the coin is submitted more than once, the bank can trace the original customer (in our previous example, Prof. Mind).

6.4 MIX AS MIX CAN

A MIX is essentially a main junction—a computer that receives messages with enciphered addresses, permutes and deciphers them, and then sends each to its intended recipient. The crucial feature in such a procedure is that the final address of the message is also enciphered, and only the MIX can decipher it. In other words, a MIX is a dedicated computer that serves for anonymity.

Figures 6.1 through 6.4 illustrate how such a process works in the nonelectronic world. One writes a message and puts it in an envelope with the address of the intended recipient. Then one puts the whole thing into a second envelope and sends it to the MIX. The MIX opens the first envelope and sends the letter to the intended recipient. (Note that this is essentially the procedure used for voting by mail.) The concept of the MIX was first presented in [Cha81]. Clearly, such a service is not for free. One would have to pay the MIX, as well as pay twice as much postage.

How can one translate this familiar system into its electronic analogue? The act of sealing a confidential message in an envelope can be simulated by enciphering the message. Note that placing the small envelope in a larger one makes the address on the small envelope invisible; consequently, in the corresponding electronic system one must also encipher the recipient's address.

A workable protocol could be based on an asymmetric encryption scheme. A sender A wants to send a message m to recipient B. In order

FIGURE 6.1

First stage: Everyone writes his letter

FIGURE 6.2

Second stage: Everyone puts his letter in a small envelope and addresses it

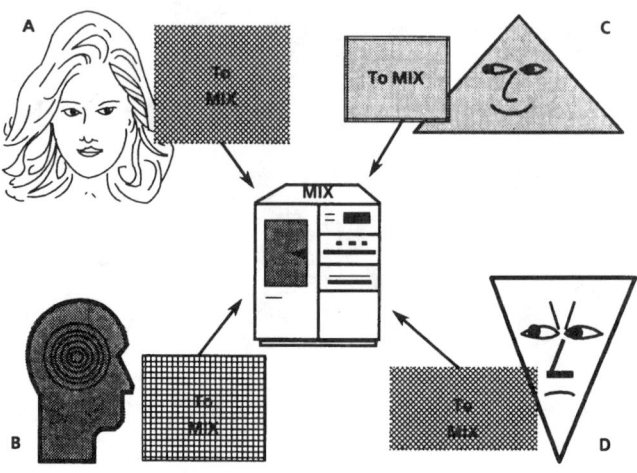

FIGURE 6.3
Third stage: Everyone puts his small envelope in a larger envelope and sends it to
the MIX

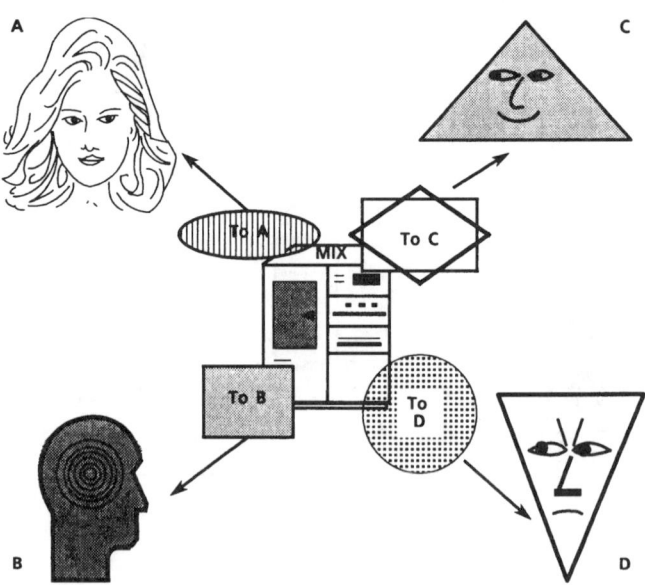

FIGURE 6.4
Fourth stage: The MIX opens the larger envelopes and sends each letter to the correct
recipient

to do so, he encrypts m together with B's address a_B using the public key E of the MIX. Thus he sends

$$E(m, a_B)$$

to the MIX. The latter is able to decipher this message using its secret key D. So, it obtains m and a_B. Therefore, the MIX can send the message m to B. Since there is no apparent relationship between a message before and after decipherment, no one has any means of tracing a messages back to its source.

Such a system can provide its desired service only if some non-cryptographic hypotheses are also valid. We note here the two most important ones.

1. The entire system fails in its purpose if very few messages are being sent at a time. It is important that there be a continual stream of many messages.

2. A serious question: Isn't it the case that everyone now must trust the MIX? In other words, hasn't the MIX become Big Brother? The answer is yes, and for this reason the use of several MIXes has been proposed; these may as well have connections with different societies (one MIX for the government, one for the trade unions, one for the consumer's society, and so on). It would then be the case that anyone could use as many MIXes as he wishes and even choose the chain of MIXes to be used.

Unfortunately, not only does the protocol become more and more complicated with multiple MIXes, but the junctions become congested bottlenecks as well.

I shall sketch the protocol for the case in which a user A wants to use two MIXes. First, he has to choose two MIXes, MIX_1 and MIX_2. Then he writes his message m along with B's address a_B and enciphers everything using MIX_2's public key E_2, yielding

$$E_2(m, a_B).$$

But A has not yet finished his work. He has to add MIX_2's address a_2 and must encipher everything using MIX_1's public key E_1; he then has

$$E_1(E_2(m, a_B), a_2)$$

and sends the whole conglomeration to MIX_1. This MIX starts the deciphering process: it obtains $E_2(m, a_B)$ and a_2. Therefore, MIX_1 knows that its duty is to forward the message $E_2(m, a_B)$ to MIX_2. The latter can now decipher everything and finally send m to B.

Any questions?

The disadvantage of such a procedure is immediately evident: every message must be enciphered several times, causing a propagation of messages that could eventually clog the MIXes. *This the price to pay for any system that offers communication anonymity!*

Additional information

How to use cryptology in order to make real money really secure. There exists a serious threat to national banks. Devices for counterfeiting banknotes are becoming continually more sophisticated and, at the same time, cheaper. Thus the advantage of the banks over the underworld continually diminishes.

Until electronic cash becomes a reality, we may as well try to improve the current system. In this regard, cryptography—in particular public key algorithms—might provide a new dimension of security (see [Omu90]). During the manufacturing process, a random pattern would be created on the banknote. This could be achieved in various ways; for instance, by a pattern made up of various particles inserted into the paper. Now this pattern is digitized into a number we'll call PAT, and varies from banknote to banknote. When manufacturing a banknote, the national bank signs PAT, meaning that it applies its secret key of a public key signature scheme. The signature SIG obtained in this way will be translated in a series of numbers SIG^*, say, and clearly printed on the banknote.

In order to verify the authenticity of a banknote, one reads SIG^*, translates this to SIG, applies the public key and obtains PAT. This information is compared to the random pattern that is read from the banknote. Of course, since banknotes are subject to the vagaries of life, one does not obtain the pristine pattern PAT, but a slightly different pattern PAT'. Now the protocol says that if PAT and PAT' coincide to within $x\%$, then the banknote is presumed to be authentic. Typical figures are $x = 80$, where PAT consists of about 3000 bits.

Note that it is not sufficient to use a signature scheme; a public key algorithm that can encipher and decipher is actually required. Also, it is crucial that SIG^* be read without any error (otherwise one would obtain no information at all); this data must be written and read in such a way that no errors occur. In other words, one must use an error-correcting code.

EXERCISES

1. Describe at least one further example from everyday life where, in your opinion, anonymity is desirable; and another example where anonymity is not desirable.

   Can you think of a situation where there are two respectable groups in society, one in favor of anonymity, the other opposed?

2. Discuss the advantages and disadvantages for a society provided by the anonymity of money. Compare this to a credit card system.

3. Choose the values for d and e of exercise 9 in chapter 5 and compute the values $111^d \bmod pq$, $222^d \bmod pq$, $333^d \bmod pq, \ldots, 777^d \bmod pq$.

4. Make precise the analogy between the scheme for electronic coins and the scheme for paper, carbon paper, and envelopes. What corresponds to C and to d?

5. Decide whether Chaum's scheme of electronic coins has the following properties. (Does ordinary money share these properties?)
   - The coin remains valid if Prof. Mind marks it a little bit.
   - The shopkeeper can use the coin and buy goods for himself.
   - The shopkeeper can submit the money only once.

6. Write down the protocol for three MIXes.

7. Determine whether a MIX (or several MIXes) could be used to solve the anonymity problem concerning key generation.

POSTSCRIPT

Before our ways diverge, I would like to share with you, gentle reader, the words of the German romantic poet Novalis (1772–1801).

His poem expresses a yearning for a world in which cryptology is no longer necessary. According to the poet, such a world will come into being as soon as man speaks the right magic word.

> If numbers and science no longer will be
> To all living creatures the critical key,
> If those who sing and kiss in the bower,
> Know more than deep thinkers in some ivory tower,
> If the people return to a life that is free
> and in the free world endeavor to be,
> If shadow and light once more and again
> Will conjoin into true clarity, then
> In the poems and tales we will recognize
> The lore of the world both ancient and wise,
> Then just one secret word will make disappear
> All that is wrong, misbegotten and drear.

(Translated by Frau Herta Holle, University of Regina)

DECIPHERING THE CIPHERTEXTS

Solutions and hints to selected exercises.

Chapter 1

Exercise 1: ... seems to have been sadly lacking in cryptographic subtlety!

Exercise 15: L & H

Exercise 20: The key is security!

Chapter 2

Exercise 6:

```
P o l y a    l p h a b    e t i c c    i p h e r
s h a v e    t h e p r    o p e r t    y t h a t
a g i v e    n c i p h    e r t e x    t l e t t
e r m a y    r e p r e    s e n t m    o r e t h
a n o n e    p l a i n    t e x t l    e t t e r.

H o w e v    e r, w e m   u s t n o    t f o r g
e t t h a    t w e n e    e d t h e    c i p h e
r t e x t    t o d e t    e r m i n    e t h e c
l e a r t    e x t u n    i q u e l    y. W e c a
n n o t, f   o r e x a    m p l e, h   a v e a n

a l g o r    i t h m i    n w h i c    h a c i p
h e r t e    x t 'X' r e  p r e s e    n t s e i
t h e r p    l a i n t    e x t 'E' o  r 'S' w i t
h o u t ...
```

Exercise 16: NO!

Chapter 5

Exercise 2: A friend of mine who read this exercise wrote to me:

You should have given a hint: The man is a second-rate mathematician! Then I would have gotten it right away. He's the French mathematician Charles P. Tebeau. Of course, it could also be the German, Albrecht E. Pause, who is is not so well known. My colleague, who is very clever at these things, argued that it must be Beulah C. Streep, the feminist author from the Bronx who ran unsuccessfully for Congress; his second guess would be Peaches Butler, a porno star from Atlanta, Georgia, suspected of having an affair with the governor.

LITERATURE

[And88] K. Andreassen, *Computer Cryptology: Beyond Decoder Rings*, Prentice-Hall, Englewood Cliffs, N.J., 1988.

[BDG88] J. L. Balcázar, J. Díaz, J. Gabarró, *Structural Complexity I*, Springer-Verlag, Heidelberg, 1988.

[BP82] H. Beker and F. Piper, *Cipher Systems: The Protection of Communication*, Northwood, London, 1982.

[BKP91] A. Beutelspacher, A. Kersten, and A. Pfau, *Chipkarten als Sicherheits-werkzeug*, Springer-Verlag, Heidelberg, forthcoming.

[Beu86] M. Beutelspacher, *Kultivierung bei lebendigem Leib*, Drumlin Verlag, Weingarten, 1986.

[BS93] E. Biham and A. Shamir, *Differential cryptanalysis of the Data Encryption Standard*, Springer-Verlag, New York, 1993.

[BDPW90] M. V. D. Burmester, Y. Desmedt, F. Piper, and M. Walker, "A general aero-knowledge scheme," in *Advances in Cryptology—Eurocrypt '89*, Springer Lecture Notes in Computer Science 434 (1990), 122–133.

[CCITT] CCITT Recommendation X.509, "The Directory—Authentication Framework," 1988.

[Cha81] D. Chaum, "Untraceable electronic mail, return addresses, and digital pseudonyms," *Communications of the ACM* 24 (1981), 84–88.

[Cha85] D. Chaum, "Security without identification: transaction systems to make Big Brother obsolete," *Communications of the ACM* 28 (1985), 1030–1044.

[CFN90] D. Chaum, A. Fiat, and M. Naor, "Untraceable electronic cash," in *Advances in Cryptology—Crypto '88*, Springer Lecture Notes in Computer Science 403 (1990), 319–327.

[Cox69] H. S. M. Coxeter, *Introduction to Geometry*, John Wiley & Sons, New York, 1969.

[DP89] D. W. Davies and W. L. Price, *Security for Computer Networks*, John Wiley & Sons, 2nd edition, 1989.

[Den83] D. Denning, *Cryptography and Data Security*, Addison Wesley, Reading, Mass., 1983.

[Dif88] W. Diffie, "The first ten years of public-key cryptography," *Proceedings of the IEEE* 76(5) (1988), 560–577.

[DH76] W. Diffie and M. E. Hellman, "New directions in cryptography," *IEEE Transactions on Information Theory*, IT-22, 6 (1976), 644–654.

[Dun90] W. Dunham, *Journey through Genius: The Great Theorems of Mathematics*, John Wiley & Sons, New York, 1990.

[ElG85] T. ElGamal, "A public key cryptosystem and a signature scheme based on discrete logarithms," *IEEE Transactions on Information Theory*, IT-31 (1985), 469–472.

[Eve80] H. Eves, *Great Moments in Mathematics (before 1650)*, Dolciani Mathematical Expositions No. 5, The Mathematical Association of America, Washington, D.C., 1980.

[FS87] A. Fiat and A. Shamir, "How to prove yourself: practical solutions to identification and signature problems," *Advances in Cryptology—Crypto '86*, Springer Lecture Notes in Computer Science 263 (1987), 186–194.

[Fra84] O. I. Franksen, *Mr. Babbage's Secret: The Tale of a Cypher—and APL*, Prentice-Hall, Englewood Cliffs, N.J., 1984.

[FP90] W. Fumy and A. Pfau, "Asymmetric authentication schemes for smart cards— dream or reality?" *Proceedings IFIP SEC '90*, Espoo, Finland.

[FR88] W. Fumy and H. P. Rieß, *Kryptographie—Entwurf und Analyse symmetrischer Kryptosysteme*, Oldenbourg, Munich, 2nd edition, 1993.

[GMR89] S. Goldwasser, S. Micali, and C. Rackoff, "The knowledge complexity of interactive proof-systems," *SIAM Journal on Computing* 8(1) (1989), 186–208.

[Gor85] J. Gordon, "Strong primes are easy to find," *Advances in Cryptology— Eurocrypt '84*, Springer Lecture Notes in Computer Science 209 (1985), 216–223.

[HW60] G. H. Hardy and E. M. Wright, *An Introduction to the Theory of Numbers*, Clarendon, Oxford, 1960.

[HDP90] P. Hawkes, D. Davies, and W. Price, *Integrated Circuit Cards, Tags and Tokens*, BSP Professional Books, Oxford, 1990.

[Hon73] R. Honsberger, *Mathematical Gems I*, Mathematical Association of America, Washington, D.C., 1973.

[ISO] ISO IS 7498/2, *Open Systems Interconnection Reference Model—Part 2: Security Architecture*.

[Kah67] D. Kahn, *The Code Breakers: The Story of Secret Writing*, Macmillan, New York, 1967.

[Kob67] N. Koblitz, *A Course in Number Theory and Cryptography*, Springer-Verlag, New York, 1987.

[Koh81] A.G. Kohnheim, *Cryptography: A Primer*, John Wiley & Sons, New York, 1981.

[Kra86] E. Kranakis, *Primality and Cryptography*, John Wiley & Sons, Chichester, 1986.

[LM90] A.K. Lenstra and M.S. Manasse, "Factoring by electronic mail," *Advances in Cryptology—Eurocrypt '89*, Springer Lecture Notes in Computer Science 434 (1990), 355–371.

[LP87] D. M. Luciano and G. D. Prichett, "Cryptology: from Caesar ciphers to public-key cryptosystems," *College Mathematics Journal*, 18 (1987), 2–17.

[Mas69] J. L. Massey, "Shift-register synthesis and BCH decoding," *IEEE Transactions on Information Theory*, IT-15, 1 (1969), 122–127.

[Mas83] J. L. Massey, "Logarithms in finite cyclic groups—cryptopgraphic issues," *Proceedings of the 4th Benelux Symposium on Information Theory* (1983), 17–25.

[Mau90] U. Maurer, "Fast generation of secure RSA-moduli with almost maximal diversity," *Advances in Cryptology—Eurocrypt '89*, Springer Lecture Notes in Computer Science 434 (1990), 636–647.

[McG90] J. McGrindle, *Smart Cards*, IFS Publications/Springer-Verlag, 1990.

[McE78] R. J. McEliece, "A public-key cryptosystem based on algebraic coding theory," JPL DSN Progress Report 42-44, pp. 114–116, Jan.–Feb., 1978.

[MH78] R.C. Merkle and M.E. Hellman, "Hiding information and signatures in trapdoor knapsacks," *IEEE Transactions on Information Theory*, IT-24 (1978), 525–530.

[MM82] C. H. Meyer and S. M. Matyas, *Cryptography: A New Dimension in Computer Data Security*, John Wiley & Sons, New York, 1982.

[Omu90] J. K. Omura, "Novel applications of cryptography in digital communications," *IEEE Communications Magazine*, May 1990, 21–29.

[OED] *The Oxford English Dictionary*

[Per86] G. Perec, *Anton Voyls Fortgang*, Zweitausendeins, Frankfurt, 1986.

[QG90] J.-J., M., M., M. Quisquater and L., M., G., A., G., S. Guillou, "How to explain zero-knowledge protocols to your children," *Advances in Cryptology—Crypto '89*, Springer Lecture Notes in Computer Science 435 (1990), 628–631.

[RSA78] R. Rivest, A. Shamir, and L. Adleman, "A method for obtaining digital signatures and public key cryptosystems," *Communications of the ACM* 21 (1978), 120–126.

[Rue86] R. Rueppel, *Analysis and Design of Stream Ciphers*, Springer-Verlag, New York, 1986.

[Sal90] A. Salomaa, *Public-Key Cryptography*, Springer-Verlag, New York, 1990.

[SP89] J. Seberry and J. Pieprzyk, *Cryptography: An Introduction to Computer Security*, Prentice-Hall, Englewood Cliffs, N.J., 1989.

[Sim92] G. J. Simmons, *Contemporary Cryptology. The Science of Information Integrity*, IEEE Press, New York, 1992.

[Sha82] A. Shamir, "A polynomial time algorithm for breaking the basic Merkle–Hellman cryptosystem," *Proceedings of the 23rd IEEE Symposium Found. Computer Sci.* (1982), 142–152.

[Sha49] C. E. Shannon, "Communication theory of secrecy systems," *Bell Systems Technical Journal* 28 (1949), 656–715.

[Smi71] L. D. Smith, *Cryptography: The Science of Secret Writing*, Dover Publications, New York, 1971.

[Str56] D. J. Struik, *A Concise History of Mathematics*, Dover Publications, New York, 1956.

Among the regular publications on cryptology three journals deserve special mention: *Journal of Cryptology* (Springer-Verlag), which has a rather scientific approach; *Computer & Security* (Elsevier), which covers not only cryptology, but also security in general; and *Cryptologia* (Rose Hulman Institute), which is also devoted to the history of cryptology.

The Springer Lecture Notes in Computer Science publish two volumes every year called *Advances in Cryptology*, namely the proceedings of the annual conferences Eurocrypt and Crypto.